AUSTRALIA II

THE OFFICIAL RECORD

A JOYCE CHILDRESS MANAGEMENT PRODUCTION

AUSTRALIA II

THE OFFICIAL RECORD

CONTENTS

FOREWORD

by Alan Bond

BEGINNINGS

Australia II blossoms from a dream into a winning reality

NEWPORT: THE RIGHT TO CHALLENGE

The crew sharpen their skills against an international elite

THE RACES

Australia II and *Liberty* meet in the best of seven series

CELEBRATIONS AND HOMECOMING

A continent stands still, then welcomes her champion crew

EPILOGUE

Predictions for the Royal Perth Yacht Club's first defence

First published in Sydney, 1984
Printed and bound in Japan for JOYCE CHILDRESS MANAGEMENT, Pty. Ltd.

© JC Management 1984

ISBN 0 9591313 0 2

14

FOREWORD

THE WINNING OF THE AMERICA'S CUP by *Australia II* at Newport, Rhode Island on September 26, 1983 was, without doubt, the sporting triumph of the century.

Even from the first elimination races at Newport the smell of success was in the air. This time, the press said, the Australians have a boat and a team that could win the Cup after 132 years of American supremacy. What the press was telling the world we had known for many months since we began testing our radically designed 12-metre in the waters off the coast of Fremantle. She was fast. She could win. Given the best possible crew and management team, we knew at last that the learning was over and our dream could become a reality.

When I first challenged with *Southern Cross* in 1974, I did not realise how much there was to learn before any challenger from a distant shore could beat the Americans with their highly-trained crews, massive financial backing and important home-water advantages. As we went into successive challenges in 1977 and 1980 we built up our expertise in many areas including our management ability to deal with any problems arising from protests, disputes and interpretations of the rules. By the time we reached our fourth challenge in 1983 we knew what it took to win.

This book is more than just a record of our fourth and successful challenge. It tells our story from the inside. Many of the photographs were taken by members of our team and show the personal side hidden from the scores of professional photographers who followed the challenge. In addition, this book shows the iron discipline and the unflinching dedication of our team, spiced with the lighter moments without which life would not have been worth living.

As far as I am concerned our win at Newport was a total team effort. From being a team of champions we became a champion team. We won the America's Cup and we brought it home to Australia.

ALAN BOND

BEGINNINGS

WHEN SIR FRANK PACKER launched Australia's first America's Cup challenge back in 1962, he was honest enough to blame his obsession with the auld mug on "alcohol and delusions of grandeur."

Alan Bond said he simply wanted to win it "for Australia."

And he did. No other event in the post-war era has had such a dramatic, galvanising effect on the Australian people.

Australia II, from her beginnings to her triumphant win in Newport, was the product of a special kind of faith; the faith of her designer Ben Lexcen in what was seen by many as an outrageous, unorthodox concept; the faith of syndicate chief Alan Bond, the man who, after all had to put up most of the money; the faith of her skipper John Bertrand and his magnificent crew and the faith, too, of the sailmakers who were experimenting with cloths and shapes as new and radical as the winged keel itself. All of these people came together and pulled as one. A small group of highly motivated, highly dedicated Australians, drawn together by a single dream, went out and took on the world's most powerful nation. *Australia II* finally 'came together' in Newport, but long before then, as far back as September 1980 and the last race of the Cup's 24th challenge, the planning had begun for what was to become the ultimate challenge. Step by careful step, like commandos planning a raid, the Australians plotted each and every move along the campaign trail.

IN SEPTEMBER 1980, Alan Bond stood on the foredeck of *Australia*'s tender watching his third America's Cup challenge go down the drain. It was the fifth and final race. Dennis Connor was steering the big blue *Freedom* to a four-one win. Bond turned to Ben Lexcen, the designer who had stuck by him with a succession of 12-metre boats and IOR yachts for over 10 years. "I want you to design me another boat," he said, "and I want John Bertrand to sail it."

There was no indication then that in three years time, they would both be standing in pretty much the same spot whooping for joy as the impossible dream came true. The ghosts of all those America's Cup greats like Mike Vanderbilt, Captain Nathaniel Herreshoff and Charlie Barr were far too numerous to suspect that yet another challenge would not go the way of all the others since 1870. But Alan Bond is a very determined man and he was very determined indeed to win the America's Cup.

Possessing the Cup, wielding the power, the influence, doing what no man had ever done, seizing yachting's Holy Grail, all these reasons and more lay behind Bond's obsession with the auld mug.

Alan Bond came to the America's Cup through what he regarded as an insult. It was in 1970 that he and Lexcen were drawn to the extraordinary sight of the new American 12-metre *Valiant* fresh from her shed at Minneford's Yard on City Island, New York. They went aboard and were promptly ejected in a very forceful way by Vic Romagna, a distinguished America's Cup crewman who ironically was to serve as secretary of the NYYC's ill-fated 1983 America's Cup committee.

Bond was so incensed at his ejection that he is said to have commissioned Lexcen on the spot to create a boat that would take the precious Cup away from New York.

Lexcen created *Southern Cross* and Bond naively tied the challenge to a resort development he was pushing at Yanchep just north of Perth. He was seen as a brash and brazen upstart by the NYYC but he had a boat, he was a member of a bona fide yacht club and they couldn't keep him out.

To be sure, before that summer was out,

Australia II one-third scale wooden model

they wished they had. *Southern Cross* lost every race but Alan Bond left a lasting impression as an aggressive competitor who did not pull his punches.

Bond came back in 1977 with another Lexcen boat. This time it was named *Australia*. She too went down four-nil. Losing is never easy especially if you have outlayed several million dollars in the confident expectation of winning. Alan Bond seemed in 1977 to be just as brash and just as aggressive and just as determined to win the Cup. He said he would come back and he did, this time with a modified *Australia* in 1980.

But, the six years since his initial challenge had changed Alan Bond. He was calmer, more secure, less prone to the verbal fisticuffs of previous campaigns. And although *Australia* went down to *Freedom* four-one, Bond set in motion the train of extraordinary events that would eventually see him triumph.

He had learned several things about America's Cup campaigning and one was that a challenger, to be successful against such consistent American excellence, had to have some technical edge either in hull design or sails, or both. He sent

Tank testing, Holland, 1981

Dr. Peter van Oossanen and Ben Lexcen

Ben Lexcen out to find them.

Lexcen took himself off to Wageningen in Holland, to the Netherlands Ship Model Basin, one of the biggest tank test facilities in the world and here, together with his wife Yvonne, he lived and worked for four intensive, creative months. He tested the very biggest models that could be towed in the tank, huge 22-footers that reduced the prospect for error to a very small degree. No one is saying precisely how much that tank test programme cost, but *Australia II*'s Executive Director Warren Jones gives a ballpark figure of $500,000 — other estimates say it was much more.

Lexcen first developed a very fast looking model of a conventional 12-metre, a refinement of the 1980 *Australia*, which would subsequently become *Challenge 12*.

But he wanted to go further. For 20 years he had been toying with the idea of wing-tipped keels. Way back in the sixties he had even gone so far as to fix wings to the bottom of the centreboard of his world champion 18-footer *Venom*. He had tinkered with glider's wings and the deadly aerodynamic efficiency of Hurricanes and Spitfires. He was convinced that wing-like appendages at the base of a keel would help negate the drag effect of the dreaded energy absorbing tip vorteces that spin around the tip of the keel from the high pressure side to the low pressure area robbing the boat of some of its potential forward force.

The ideas that came tumbling out of his brain were fed into a computer generator at the Dutch International Aerospace Laboratories in Amsterdam and it was here on a video display terminal, that he saw for the first time all those crazy notions were not only soundly based, but offered the potential for the kind of quantum leap that Bond was so desperately looking for.

Lexcen telephoned Warren Jones. "Benny was very excited," Jones remembers. "He said he was convinced he was on to something really big, something really significant, a breakthrough. Could I send more money? How much more money? $50,000." "It had better be a big breakthrough," warned Jones.

Jones remained sceptical until he flew to Holland to see the numbers for himself. It was a breakthrough. The next step was to convince

Bond to forget the conventional and opt for the radical, the untried, the revolutionary notion of a winged keel.

Bond and John Bertrand were in Cowes campaigning for the Admiral's Cup. Jones picked them up in a chartered jet and they flew to Holland.

"I remember looking at it," Bond recalled, "and I thought this thing will either be a submarine that will take us all to the bottom or it will help us win the Cup. I decided it was worth a try." The decision to go ahead was actually taken during the flight back to Cowes. Lexcen stayed on at Wageningen to build three 22-foot models that would be modified many times before the final shape was proven. It was in fact the hull design made possible by the winged keel and not the foil configuration itself which gave *Australia II* its superior performance. Once Lexcen had hit upon the correct angle of attack for the wings, he found they acted not only as an effective end plate but provided such a significant improvement to the keel's lift coefficient that it allowed him to reduce the hull's underbody in the forefront and bustle and thus lessen drag-inducing wetted area as well as displacement.

Casting the wings in lead, which added three tons right at the base of the keel, lowered the centre of gravity by 95cm over a conventional 12-metre so she was stiffer and more stable in a seaway. *Australia II* would also sail closer to the wind than any other Twelve, she would accelerate out of tacks faster than her heavier conventional counterparts and thanks to the reduced underwater volume within her slender hull she had the agility and nimbleness of an aquatic ballerina.

Western Australia's master boatbuilder, Steve Ward, started lofting *Australia II*'s lines in October, 1981. She rolled out of his Cottesloe shed in May, 1982. From the outset, the keel was enveloped in an opaque plastic sheath. Both Bond and Lexcen were afraid the Americans would copy it if they got even half way accurate photographs. The Americans did in fact get pictures in Newport, but by that time it was too late to duplicate the keel.

While the keel had obvious benefits, it also had its drawbacks and these, in retrospect, were not without their humorous side. During the

yacht's sail up the coast from Perth in company with *Challenge 12* there were all sorts of dismayed looks from her crew when under spinnaker *Challenge* simply waltzed away from her.

"We couldn't understand it," Warren Jones said. "*Challenge* left us for dead. She had to hang about and wait for us to catch up and when we did she would go off again. We thought we had fallen for a real pup." But some bright spark hit upon the rather desperate notion that the radical forward sloping keel might have snagged some of the heavy weed that infests the coastal waters. The crew turned the boat into the wind and sailed her backwards. From beneath the bows emerged an enormous clump of sea grass.

The weed was such a headache off Perth and Fremantle that Colin Beashel, the brilliant young Sydney sailor who was to become her mainsheet trimmer, invented a knotted line that was keel-hauled under the bows every time she went to sea.

In Newport she faced similar hassles with lobster pots. On two occassions, once against *Azzurra* and the other against *Advance*, *Australia II* snagged her keel on the long lines that connect the pots on the ocean floor with the floating buoys on the surface. On both occassions the rope left deep gouge marks through the yacht's microballoon skin and into the lead on the keel.

Sailtrimmer Robbie Brown remembers the lobster pot incident in the race against the Italians because that's the day *Azzurra* beat *Australia II*. "We lee bowed them and then stopped," he said. "They just sailed right over the top of us. They were cock-a-hoop of course because they thought they had our number. But we could feel the boat slow down. In one and a half minutes of dragging the pot our speed dropped down by one and a half knots. From then on we formed a Lobster Pot Watch. The call would come back: 'Pot on the bow, come up or bear away.' We weaved all over the place avoiding lobster buoys."

One of the most important members of the *Australia II* crew, perhaps even *the* most important, never sailed in any race. He stayed ashore, mostly on the telephone arguing with the New York Yacht Club and dealing with the hundreds of journalists like me who pestered him from sunup to sundown. Warren Jones was *Australia*

II's executive director. But he was much, much more than that. He was *Australia II*'s saviour. He was the tough negotiator, the politician, the shrewd, calculating self-styled 'corporate brawler' who carefully chartered a course for the Australian challenge and successfully steered it through one of the most turbulent periods in America's Cup history. Warren Jones is the man American skipper Dennis Connor said should be Australian Prime Minister.

Jones told the crew: "you fight your battles on the water and let me fight those on shore." That effectively removed the keel controversy from the crew's domain. Since they didn't have to worry about the battle with the NYYC, they got on with the job of sailing to win. Jones was always articulate, sensitive and persuasive and if ever he gives up his job as a director of the Bond Corporation, I suggest he would be an excellent Ambassador in some international trouble spot. "Everyone respected Warren," Colin Beashel said. "We were happy to leave the arguments to him because that took a lot of the media pressure off the crew. When the press was busy concentrating on the keel controversy, they were not focusing on us the way they had in past challenges. That allowed us to perfect our techniques without copping a barrage of criticism in the papers."

It was *Australia II*'s father figure, the sage Sir James Hardy who advised the crew not to read the newspapers. "You're making the news," he said, "there's no need to read about yourselves."

Sir James was right. A lot of the journalists who turned up in Newport could scarcely recognise the sharp end from the blunt end. Some of the more sensational tabloids, not only in Australia but in Britain and the US as well concentrated on the negative. If people in Australia were prepared to lynch the America's Cup Committee (and some of them certainly sent obscene letters to committee members) it was perhaps because, with the single exception of *The Age*, not one newspaper sought to present the NYYC point of view. I did and I found it a very persuasive one. John Bertrand did too. After the series he wrote that their point of view was "quite legitimate and logical."

Over 200 men applied for the 11 crew positions aboard *Australia II*. Only 60 were asked to try out. That selection process took over six months and was conducted by John Longley, the syndicate manager who took the crew candidates racing aboard Alan Bond's 53-foot ocean racer *Apollo III*. By the time the boat was launched in May 1982, Longley had the nucleus of the racing crew. They were men from every state in Australia with the single exception of the Northern Territory. They were told, in very blunt terms that they would need to sacrifice all else to the success of the 12-metre campaign.

"We told them they had to be 100 per cent dedicated to winning the Cup," Warren Jones said, "or else they ought to forget all about it."

"If there were family problems, business problems, anything that stood between us and the Cup, then they were told to forget it. It was a ruthless approach, but it was necessary. We couldn't allow men who were less than totally dedicated to wriggle in among men who were giving up everything. They would stand out and there would be trouble. As it turned out, we came up with the most 'single-minded', the most determined, the fittest and the most skilled bunch of 12-metre yachtsmen ever to leave Australia."

The crew were subjected to commando style intensive training periods in which they plunged into the almost obsessive quest for physical and mental fitness. These ITP's lasted nine days at a time and gave those who had not sailed in a previous Cup campaign, a taste of what life in Newport was all about. Warren Jones and John Longley organised what they called a "total simulation" exercise when *Australia II* went to Melbourne for the Westpac regatta series throughout January, February and March. The entire crew moved into the old Customs House near the Royal Yacht Club of Victoria at Williamstown, set up their living quarters, their offices and their containers full of tools and sails and lived for three months just as they would under actual Cup campaign conditions. That was the sort of preparation that put *Australia II* head and shoulders above the other Cup contenders. By the time they were ready to leave for the real showdown at Newport they were as well prepared as they could have been. Even so, they recognised they still had a lot to learn. That realisation turned out to be one of their greatest strengths.

An initial step in building any yacht is 'lofting the lines', at left, where the curved shapes of the hull are laid out on a floor plan. The fine adjustment, by hand, of these gentle curves is part of the art of boatbuilding. Once this is done, cross-section frames or ribs, below, can be shaped and aligned, giving the hull its strength and form.

In *Australia II*, above, the hull was made of aluminium alloy sheets welded to an aluminium frame, then painstakingly smoothed over with microballoons, a tough epoxy paste, before painting. Even in these early stages of building at Steve Ward's boatsheds in the Perth suburb of Cottesloe, the winged keel is carefully concealed in a plywood box.

After eight months, *Australia II* emerges from her Cottesloe birthplace as project manager John Longley, designer Ben Lexcen, Steve Ward and the building team look on. Her design was so innovative, no one was really sure how the yacht would perform. Alan Bond suggested she would either be a 'submarine' that would take them all to the bottom, or she would win the America's Cup. After a short road trip to Fremantle, *Australia II* would have her first taste of salt water on the third of June, 1982.

Three days after the launch, on Founders' Day, Eileen
Bond christens *Australia II* at the Fremantle Sailing Club
in Success Harbour. The new yacht, surrounded by
secrecy, was already attracting a loyal following.
Western Australian Governor, Admiral Sir Richard
Trowbridge hoped, in his christening speech that "here
in this brand new gleaming white hull . . . at long last
Mr. Alan Bond and Australia have got a winner." Alan
Bond was even more confident. The new yacht, he said
had "the highest technology of any 12-metre in the
world". He continued, "Obviously, I can't tell you about
the secrets, but they're there . . .After 131 years, the
Americans have gradually lost their advantage; we, on
our part, have narrowed the gap. For the first time, we'll
go into this competition, I believe, on an equal footing.
There should be no excuses for defeat." It is likely that
prospective America's Cup yachts the world over begin
their careers this way, only to end up in the charter
business twelve months later. *Gretel,* for example, which
shocked the Americans in 1962 by actually winning a
race, is now working in the Whitsunday Passage and
Dame Pattie, Australia's 1967 challenger, was sold to a
Canadian and now works as an ocean racer. But not this
time — *Australia II* was on her way into sporting history.

The strong winds and big seas off Fremantle were perfect proving-grounds for the newly launched *Australia II*. During winter and spring trials, numerous adjustments to the boat were made, including a re-positioning of the keel 23cm forward. Prospective crew members were tested as well, but real competition was yet to come, at the Westpac Advance Australia Cup in Melbourne.

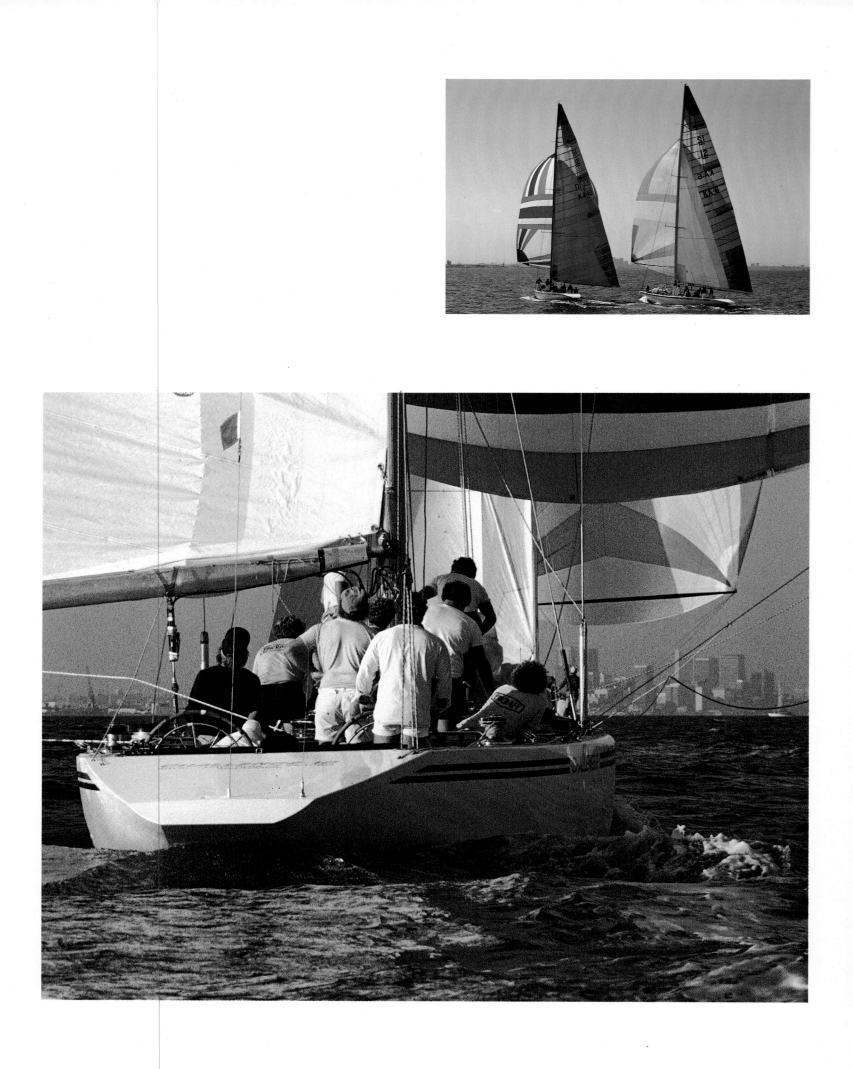

Port Phillip Bay can be very similar to Newport in late summer with a slight swell and gentle winds. The Westpac Advance Australia Cup series gave two of the new Australian challengers, *Australia II*, and *Challenge 12*, an opportunity to race each other and also try themselves against previous challenger *Gretel II*. Unfortunately at the last moment, *Advance* was not able to travel to Victoria due to a major work programme on her hull.

Australia II won the Westpac Advance Australia Cup convincingly. While Alan Bond and John Bertrand display the Cup, the crew poses with their summer mascot, Shadow. At right, the crew is presented with the Westpac spanner.

NEWPORT
THE RIGHT TO CHALLENGE

Throughout their long build-up in Australian waters, the crew of *Australia II* played at war games. They were 'psyched' into mock battles in which they imagined their Melbourne rival, *Challenge 12*, was in fact the dreaded Yankee Cup defender. They learned to suffer and yes, even enjoy the aching, heart-pounding thrill of close tacking duels and constant gybing. Muscles developed but so too did a mental preparedness. A team spirit, a oneness developed. Sailing mates grew into friends and there developed an emotional bond, not only between the men but between the men and the boat. *Australia II* developed her own personality. She was 'the great little boat,' or 'the fighter.' She was patted, hugged and even kissed. No thoroughbred racehorse ever received more pampered attention than the big white yacht with the bold green and gold cove stripe and the leaping green kangaroos at her bows. All these new skills were to prove essential for the critical move to Newport where the war games stopped and the real battle began. No group of Australian yachtsmen (one might even suggest no group of Australian sportsmen) has ever been as well prepared for the task of winning. Their experience must serve as a benchmark for all those who come later.

AUSTRALIA II's advance party, John Longley, Ken Beashel and his son Colin, Phil Smidmore and the Royal Perth Yacht Club's distinguished and highly skilled former Commodore John Fitzhardinge, arrived in Newport about mid-May. Their first job was to erect the plywood and green canvas security screen around the berth at Newport Offshore. It was an ingenious Heath Robinson style device with all manner of pulleys and lead counterweights designed to draw the curtain tight around the great white hull as she was hauled vertically out of the water each night after racing. The curtain was never intended to be a permanent fixture, but as the Australians realised how potent a psychological weapon the secret was, the more determined they became to keep the curtains intact. Like brothers protecting their kid sister's innocence, they became fiercely jealous of anyone who so much as uttered a disparaging word against her. By the time the main body of crewmen arrived at the end of May, the yacht had been safely towed from New York, rigged and test sailed by the advance men. The advance party had also set up the all important workshop area, a 40-foot container crammed with all the gear they would need to maintain the boat in top racing form. They had drill presses, a lathe, a milling machine and grinding wheels all in the container. Another 20-foot container was used as a sail storage bin and as a repository for all their running rigging. It was in the bowels of this container that the tall, elegant figure of Commodore Fitzhardinge could be seen most mornings at six, patiently splicing the Kevlar line that Australia II used exclusively as her running rigging. 'Fitzy', as he was known affectionately by everyone, became so adept at the intricate Kevlar splices, he even invented several of his own. None of them ever gave way and the use of Kevlar saved Australia II carrying nearly 100 kg of wire gear around the race course.

Very few other sporting events anywhere in the world place so many demands on competing foreign crews as does the America's Cup. Time (four long and exhausting months), distance (16,000 km) and an intense and often strange and indeed strained environment often add up to miserable bouts of homesickness.

And when things don't go right, questions begin to arise: 'Why ARE we here? Is a boat race worth all the hassle? Is there life after the America's Cup?' In 1983, those questions and others were posed, not merely by those who had come so far to sail aboard Australia II, the Melbourne boat Challenge 12 and the Sydney boat Advance, but also by the Italians, the French, the Canadians and the British. My experience in Newport throughout the summer of '83 showed that only two syndicates, Australia II and the Italians aboard Azzurra, ever really found the answers. Motivation was at least as powerful a weapon in Newport as the sails that drove the boats. The man behind the Australia II crew's racing motivation was her skipper, John Bertrand. Bertrand had earned a Master's degree in Ocean Engineering from Boston's prestigious M.I.T. with a thesis on the aerodynamics of 12-metre sails, and was the epitome of the supercool high-tech whiz kid. Laconic, almost to the point of being taciturn, Bertrand built a tremendous rapport with every man aboard, simply by being a thorough professional. The crew respected his judgement and he respected theirs. But above all, Bertrand was seen to be his own man. He had a good relationship with Alan Bond, but he did not jump merely because Bondy said so.

Bertrand was a great pusher. Even after a long, hard day of racing, he still found the energy to stay out there and look at sails. There might have been a few grumbles at the time, but everyone realised it was the very best thing that could have been done.

Outside Founders Hall, the great rambling grey shingle crew house on Ruggles Avenue, at 6.30 each morning, rigorous exercise was a daily ritual, race or no race, rain, hail or shine. For 45 minutes, every member of the crew (and sometimes even the bleary eyed sailmakers who had worked all night) ran about four kilometres and did push ups and sit ups.

The exercises were under the direction of Carlton Football Club's sports psychologist Laurie Hayden. Hayden divided the crew into two teams, (port and starboard) in an attempt to instill the sort of genuine aggression that could later be taken out on the opposition. These

Liberty Crew Residence; Seaview Terrace, Ruggles Avenue

"aggro games" of football and soccer succeeded too well, they became such hostile encounters, that in the end, Volleyball had to be substituted.

During their daily runs, the *Australia II* crew sometimes passed the *Freedom-Liberty* crew head-quarters, another sprawling old house with vast lawns. The Aussies were bold enough to run around the *Freedom* lawn and on one occasion, to use it for their exercises. Just to make sure the Americans knew they were out there and working hard, the Australians added a clap between each of their push ups.

The Yanks came out after them once, and in a good natured tussel, ran among them tackling and barging like a pack of gridiron footballers. After all this exercise, the crew showered and came down to a breakfast, that in the early weeks consisted of American style pancakes and maple syrup, the kind of food guaranteed to undo all the good road work they had just endured.

It was the food that was taken aboard the boat during the day that really gave them trouble. Day after day the crews were faced with the same inedible American sandwiches, fashioned from ghastly plastic bread. The orange juice was invariably frozen and more often than not, the lunches went overboard rather than into the crew. They came to dread the daily opening of their lunch boxes and it was only toward the end of their Cup campaign that regular Australian style salads appeared in individual bowls.

People who read about the Newport social whirl and perhaps saw the old Grace Kelly, Bing Crosby, Frank Sinatra movie 'High Society' imagined that the racing crews must have been having a fine time. Nothing could have been further from the truth. There were several magnificent balls and dinners, but after a long day at sea and all those relentless early morning exercises, the crew scarcely had enough strength left to peddle home on their bicycles, let alone get gussied up to go out on the town. They usually contented themselves with dinner together at the crew house, a few drinks, then into bed before 10 p.m.

On the other hand, people who knew the behaviour of other Australian America's Cup crews in Newport, were quite frankly surprised at the level of serious dedication and sheer professionalism in the *Australia II* crew. Seven of them had been through the Cup mill before, so they knew the only way to beat the Americans was

41

to knuckle down to a 100 per cent effort, and if that meant curbing their social instincts for three months, then it had to be. That the *Australia II* boys took themselves seriously there is no doubt, but there was a humorous side to their professionalism, too.

It was Colin Beashel and sailtrimmer Robbie Brown who came up with the idea of "red carding" crewmen who offended the professional dignity of the cup campaign after a John Bertrand outburst against Brown early in the summer. Bertrand was not satisfied with the headsail trim and he blew Brown up in front of the entire crew. The incident was so unsettling, that the following morning the crew filed back to the helmsman's position to hang the first red card around their skipper's neck. "Everyone laughed," Brown recalled. "It was a mellow way of telling the guy to shut-up. It had the most significant effect in calming the whole crew down. John didn't say a word all day and we sailed one of the best races we had all summer." In soccer of course, rule infringements are noted on a referee's card. Persistent offenders are liable to be tossed off the field. The red card, about the size of a cigarette pack and emblazoned with a smiling face and the message "Have a Nice Day" was hung around the neck of anyone who swore or behaved in a beligerent way toward his crewmates. The offending crewman was "put on trial" during dinner when he had to listen to his accusers launch a good natured "prosecution." A defence could be entered, but since it was the crew who passed judgement, the verdict was invariably "guilty." The card was worn until someone else earned the right to wear it.

The business of 12-metre match racing absorbed a tremendous amount of mental as well as physical energy, and because no one could be expected to tune their brain to the total demands of racing all the time, the Australians developed a switching system as a means of either relaxing or throwing the full weight of their concentration into their racing. If someone said: "OK, the switch is ON," that meant the boat was in full racing mode. If the switch was said to be OFF, that meant they were in their cruising mode and could relax.

But there was little time for relaxing. The

challenge eliminations were conducted with only a few minor breaks throughout June, July and August. There were six other Cup contenders in Newport and no matter how badly they sailed, *Australia II* still had to go through the motions of racing them. It was a long and tedious process and yet with each outing, the *Australia II* crew learned more and more about their own strengths and weaknesses.

Australia II continued her triumphant march through eight of the nine semi-final races in a series of light, moderate and on rare occasions, fresh breezes. Earlier in the mainly light airs of the preliminary A, B, C round-robin series of 40 races, she scored 36 wins against her six rivals. These included seven wins over the British boat *Victory '83*, six each over *Canada 1*, the Italian boat *Azzurra*, the Royal Sydney Yacht Squadron's contender *Advance* and *France 3* and five over *Challenge 12*, the Melbourne boat.

There was never any question, in my mind at least, that *Australia II* would be the eventual challenger. And although the competition she faced could not be compared with the cut-throat, short tacking, windward and return approach adopted by the autocrats of the NYYC selection committee, the Australians were nevertheless able to learn a little from each opponent. It was the Italians who taught them about downwind spinnaker handling, pole positions, angles and shapes. "The Italians taught us a lot about square running in particular," Colin Beashel said. "Everybody from Dennis Conner on down thought we were sandbagging, but we weren't. We were just plain slow because we were still learning how to handle the boat best downhill. We liked what we saw on the Italian boat so much, that we video taped their spinnaker handling techniques and tried to copy them." The Italians were very good, but their inexperience in big boat match racing told against them. They emerged as the real danger, along with the Americans for the first Australian defence effort in 1987.

The Canadians, with the young and aggressive Terry McLaughlin at the helm, were especially good at starts. Bertrand and Treharne were always on their toes against McLaughlin before the gun, but after the start the Australians had little trouble in disposing of the Canadians. Inexperience, a lack of money and subsequently poor quality sails meant their effort was doomed from the start. The British showed there was more to match racing than sticking to the textbook theory that says you must stay between your opponent and the mark. The British skippers, Lawrie Smith and Rodney Pattison were quick to realise they could neither tack nor point with *Australia II*, so they sailed off looking for the shifts. Playing the shifts was a strategy Dennis Conner would be forced to use when *Liberty* came up against the Australians in the Cup finals.

The French were not much help to *Australia II*. Bruno Trouble was a very talented helmsman, and although he was usually full of fire and attack at the starts, all his moves were fairly predictable. The Australians tended to regard races against the French more in the nature of a sail testing exercise.

The *Australia II* crew regarded the *Challenge 12* men as over-confident. It was a view which was unfortunately shared by many of us who watched the summer campaign unfold. The crew from the Royal Yacht Club of Victoria did have what seemed to many observers, an unjustified sense of their own potential. They were going to win the America's Cup and nothing was going to stand in their way. Instead of learning from the *Australia II* crew, who were after all the most experienced of all the foreign contenders, they tried silly tactics like trying to "psych" them out by deliberately ignoring their fellow countrymen with whom they shared a dock. Relations between the two Australian camps deteriorated and that did not help anyone. When *Challenge 12* became *Australia II*'s trial horse, Mike Fletcher, the Australian Olympic coach, Damian Fewster, the bowman and David Wallace, the maintenance fitter, were the only crewmen invited to stay on and join the Royal Perth campaign. *Challenge 12* was crewed by the men from *Advance*. I stress the word men. They came to the United States as a raw bunch of boys with very little 12-metre experience, but by the end of the summer they showed such unflagging dedication and prodigious capacity for work, that they certainly earned the right to take a full share of the credit for *Australia II*'s great win.

But while *Australia II* was busy demolishing the other contenders for challenge honours, the NYYC was busy trying to demolish *Australia II*. In an unprecedented campaign that lasted over two months, the club's most senior officers tried on the one hand to suggest the radical winged keel was unfairly rated, that it was illegal and ought to be either modified or disqualified. Then, on the other hand, they set about trying to purchase a copy for their own use.

And when all that failed, a concerted attempt was made to suggest Ben Lexcen was not the true designer of *Australia II*, and that the winged keel was in fact the product of a Dutch design team led by Dr. Peter van Oossanen.

It was a row that rivalled even the notorious Dunraven affair, for the bitterness and anger it engendered. Any notion that the America's Cup was a purely sporting event was forever tossed out the window. After several unsuccessful pleas to have the winged keel brought before the all powerful International Yacht Racing Union's Keelboat Committee, the NYYC was at last forced to concede defeat when the British syndicate chief, Peter de Savary produced a ruling given to his own designer Ian Howlett by an IYRU sub-committee in 1982 giving the green light to winged appendages. De Savary never properly explained why he remained silent about that permission for so long. But in doing so, he allowed the NYYC to wade into a dreadfully sticky pit.

The NYYC went through the motions of conducting Defence Trials, but it was clear from the outset that their favourite boat was Dennis Conner's *Liberty*. Conner, one of the most gifted 12-metre helmsmen in the world, was the man they were convinced would retain the cup. After all, had he not given three years of his life to the single minded pursuit of precisely that goal?

The Club was right. Conner *was* the best man for the job. Although he had a slower boat he would, through sheer sailing skill, drag the 25th challenge for the America's Cup out to a 3-3 sudden death sail off and come within a hair's breadth of holding it.

What is a 12-metre?

Think of it not so much as a boat, but a cocktail. Mix together a little waterline length and a touch of sail area, add a dash of beam and a draft and stir over lots and lots of cold cash. Continue stirring (this is important) for around three months, then presto, if all this measures 12-metres, you've got yourself an America's Cup campaigner. It also helps if you begin by being a naval architect who understands the relationship between calculus, politics, boat owners' egos and mental exhaustion. If all that sounds frightfully complex, the actual 12-metre equation is a relatively simple mathematical formula.

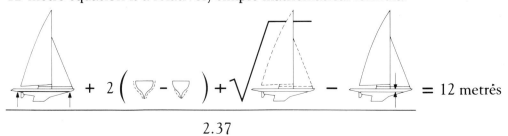

Yachts shall comply in every respect with the requirements regarding construction and equipment contained in the Deed of Gift and the Interpreting Resolutions applying to national origin of design and construction.

Bilges shall be kept as reasonably dry as possible while racing. No devices shall be fitted or employed which would permit the tilting of the mast athwartship.

The Twelve-Metre Class of racing sailboats is based on a quotient of the following formula that equals 12 metres, or 39.37 feet.

$$\frac{L + 2d + \quad SA - F}{2.37} = R$$

    $L =$ Length of the hull measured approximately 7 inches above the load waterline. Corrections for girth are applied to this measurement.

    $d =$ The skin girth is measured on the surface of the hull from sheet to keel about midships. The chain girth measured at the same place is the length of line stretched taut from the sheer to the keel and is deducted from the skin girth to give the d component.

  $SA =$ Sail area includes the mainsail and the fore triangle bounded by the mast, forestay, and deck.

    $F =$ Freeboard, or height of hull above waterline.

 2.37 = The mathematical constant.

    $R =$ Rating (12 metres in this class).

Sir James Hardy, skipper in three previous Australian challenges, was team advisor and back-up skipper of *Australia II*. During 11 elimination races, when John Bertrand was resting a cricked neck, Sir James drove *Australia II* to victory. His calm and experience proved invaluable as the situation at Newport tensed up during the late summer.

John Bertrand and Alan Bond relax on deck in the early days at Newport. The Round Robin elimination series did not begin until mid-June.

Design 'break-throughs' in 12-metre yachts are rare. The American defender, *Intrepid,* was a 1967 example and although Australian challenger *Dame Pattie* was a magnificent boat, it was out of its league. Ben Lexcen designed a 'break-through' boat with *Australia II.* And although the idea of a winged keel was not new, the computer analysis of the design and the exhaustive tank testing was. Lexcen found the angles on the wing were so critical that slight changes greatly reduced performance. No one had thought to refine the wings — doing so broke 132 years of Cup domination.

John Longley, or 'Chink' as he is known to the crew, was project manager of the *Australia II* challenge. A veteran of the three previous Bond efforts in *Southern Cross* and *Australia* (twice), his role this time was supposed to be managerial. However, he was included in the crew as either the mastman or one of the grinders during the racing at Newport.

PREVIOUS PAGE   The Newport docks await a thirsty spectator fleet heading in from the racing in Rhode Island Sound.

Bowman Scott McAllister, who broke his arm later in the series, changes a headsail during sail testing.

The three elimination series, called round robin A, B and C, were run between the French, Italians, Canadians, British and Australians. Racing regularly from mid-June to August, crews honed their skills to the competitive edge needed for a successful challenge. Endless hours of practice and constant racing betwen contenders took their toll and it soon became clear which boats were the fastest.

Sydney designer Alan Payne, with two great 12-metre yachts to his credit (*Gretel* and *Gretel II*), was commissioned to build two more for Syd Fischer's 12-metre syndicate. Challenging through the Royal Sydney Yacht Squadron, the syndicate wanted a pair of 12's to train together in Australia, then ship the best one to Newport for a shot at the Cup.

However, while the first was under construction, the syndicate ran short of funds and Payne put all his innovative design ideas into one radical boat. *Advance* was crewed by a young, enthusiastic bunch of Sydney sailors with five time 18-footer champion Iain Murray as their skipper, but she remained an unresponsive performer and won only two races all summer.

The America's Cup elimination series, where a single boat wins the right to challenge for the Cup, is a long, trying campaign testing skill, stamina and patience to the limit. One of the many aspects of *Australia II*'s success was the attitude of her crew. They knew winning must be a total team commitment and everyone worked to that end. Many of the crew were sailing champions in their own right, competing internationally up to Olympic level, but in order to insure overall success, individual rivalries had to be put aside for the common good.

The *Australia II* syndicate office was the hub of the entire operation in Newport. It was in this rickety, old, two-room boatshed on the Newport Offshore dock that telephones rang, telexes chattered, photocopiers hummed and the media harassed 13 hours every day for most of the summer. Race Co-ordinator John Fitzhardinge, Syndicate Executive Director Warren Jones, and Office Manager Alison Baker, lean over the custom-built 'press barrier' while Public Relations Officer Lesleigh Green relaxes inside. "We had a love-hate relationship with the place," Lesleigh recalled. "We could see Christie's Restaurant from our front door and it was sometimes really depressing to see everyone enjoying themselves across the street while we were working late; but occasionally someone would take pity on us and bring a drink over." But the press corps used to watch from Christie's with equal interest. Lights burning late at the office often meant a story was breaking.

Security at the *Australia II* dock was tight from the beginning. Safeguarding the keel was paramount, but keeping the large crowds away from the crew's work area soon became a major consideration. Maintenance is a mammoth task with 12-metre yachts. They are designed as light racing craft not endurance machines, and with four boats, *Australia II*, *Challenge 12*, *Azzurra* and *France 3* all side by side, the crews alone were pressed for space; curious on-lookers had to keep their distance.

The Italian boat, *Azzurra,* was one of the surprise successes of the elimination series. It was the Italians first challenge yet this sleek racing machine was one of the few boats to beat *Australia II* in an elimination race and ended the series third overall. *France 3* and *Advance* were not as fortunate, both were eliminated early in the series. *Challenge 12* followed soon after, but another first try entrant, *Canada 1,* survived to finish fourth overall. The British entrant, *Victory '83,* despite considerable unrest within their sydnicate, survived the elimination series to meet *Australia II* in the finals.

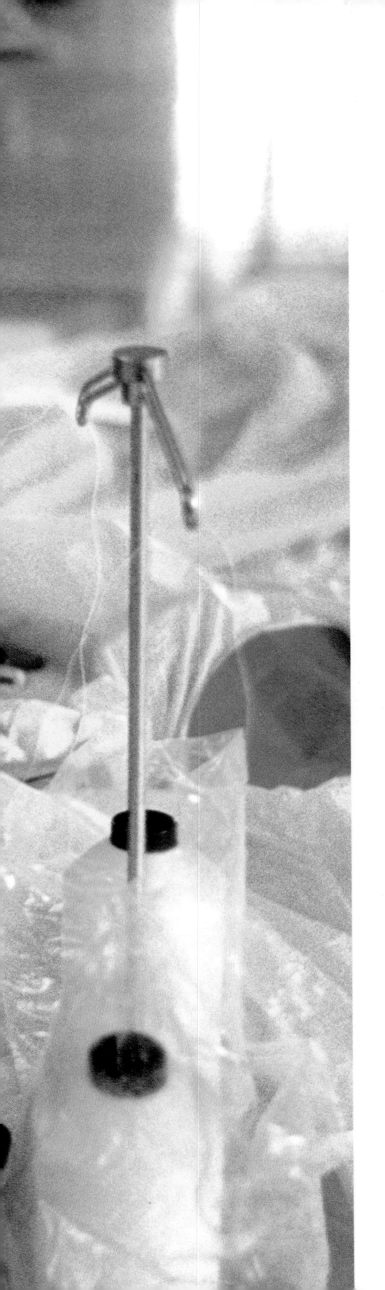

One of *Australia II*'s great advantages over *Liberty* was the quality of her sails. Tom Schnackenberg, top, was *Australia II*'s sail co-ordinator responsible for computer analysis and development of the suit of sixty sails available in Newport. The sails were made by a team of five sailmakers including Mike Quilter, left, who often sewed through the night to have adjustments or repairs done in time for sailing the next day. Sailtrimmers like Rob Brown, above, besides actively trimming headsails, were responsible for sail selection, check for damage, and calling boatspeed to the helmsman.

No West Australian challenge for the America's Cup would be complete without Former Royal Perth Yacht Club Commodore John Fitzhardinge, left. Beside his regular duties, 'Fitzy' was *Australia II*'s rigger, responsible for all the kevlar splicing aboard.

Both Tactician Hugh Treharne, above, and Sailtrimmer Skip Lissiman, below, are veterans of previous challenges. Treharne was on *Southern Cross* in 1974 and Lissiman was sailtrimmer on *Australia* in 1980. This depth of experience in the crew was another telling factor in *Australia II*'s success.

Ken Beashel, left, was maintenance chief of *Australia II*. Before and after each race, the yacht was checked from stem to stern and keel to masthead. Breakage problems on a racing boat the size and weight of *Australia II* were not uncommon, so maintenance was constant and often went on throughout the night before an important race.

In a comparison of old and new navigational aids, Bowman Damian Fewster holds a sextant at left while Grinder Will Baillieu points a hand bearing compass. Primitive sextants guided Columbus and Magellan, while modern 12-metre yachts use the luger-like hand bearing compass, pointed at buoys or other yachts, to give a digital read out of compass bearing.

The Americans spent the summer sorting out their Cup defenders. Dennis Conner, backed by the powerful Fort Schuyler Maritime Academy, campaigned with the shiny new *Liberty*. A syndicate from Texas entered the old, reliable *Courageous*. She successfully defended against Bond's first two challenges *Southern Cross* and *Australia*. But the only thing about *Courageous* was her name. The entire boat was rebuilt and she pushed *Liberty* to the limit in the defenders' trials.

Defender was the product of a New York syndicate including Tom Blackaller, starting helmsman of passed-over 1980 Cup defender, *Clipper*. He hoped *Defender* would give him a chance against Californian Dennis Conner, the successful 1980 skipper in *Freedom*. *Defender* proved very fast in early trials, but when brought to Newport for official measurement, her boom and waterline length were both too long. When these were shortened, she lost her competitive edge along with her chances to defend the America's Cup.

Dennis Conner campaigned hard for the 1983 defence. It was not by accident that he was the most successful 12-metre skipper in history, and he needed a boat faster than his old, reliable *Freedom*. In 1982, he ordered two new 12-metre yachts, *Magic* and *Spirit*. When neither could match *Freedom* he ordered a third, hopefully combining the good points of the first two. *Liberty* was more to Conner's liking and after a hard summer's match racing against the other contenders and his trial horse, *Freedom*, Conner received the traditional dockside visit by the NYYC Committee to confer the right to defend the America's Cup.

Freedom has wings grafted on her keel in an attempt to match *Australia II*'s speed and give more competition to *Liberty*. No one thought this a particularly serious threat, since the exact size and angle of the wings for *Australia II* took Ben Lexcen many months of calculation, trial and error to figure out.

Despite a few set-backs during the eliminations, including a broken boom in a race against *Azzurra*, *Australia II* fared very well. After the elimination races were complete, her record was 48 victories to only 6 defeats. This meant she and the runner-up, British entrant *Victory '83*, would meet in the elimination finals.

The elimination finals were a brief affair, but they began with a great surprise when *Australia II* lost the first race. Newport buzzed, maybe she wasn't as fast as all the media experts said. The press shot back that the Australians were sail testing during the first meeting instead of racing. But the next four races, which *Australia II* won handily, proved the media pundits correct.

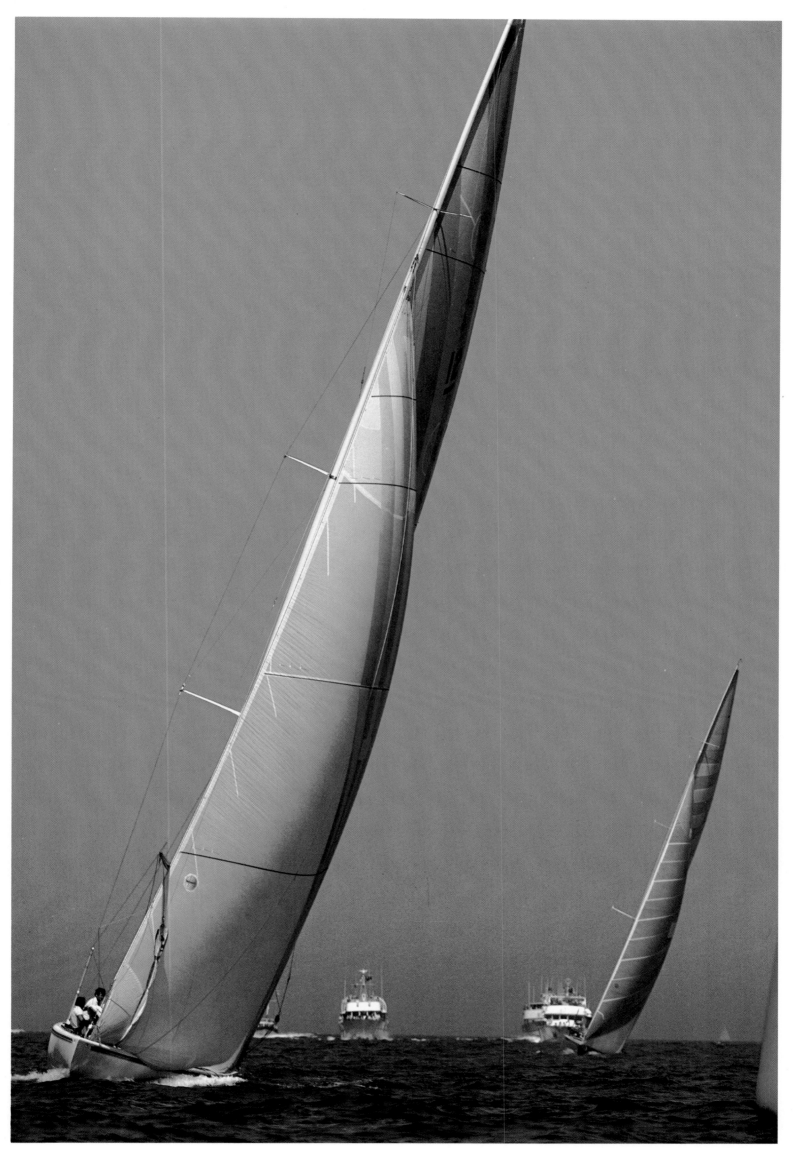

Australia II's decisive victories over *Victory '83* added to the worries of the
NYYC Race Committee. This Australian challenger was the quickest, most
manoeuvrable 12-metre ever seen on Rhode Island Sound, and their only hope
for a successful 1983 Cup defence now lay in the hands of Dennis Conner, his
new boat and his legendary bag of tricks.

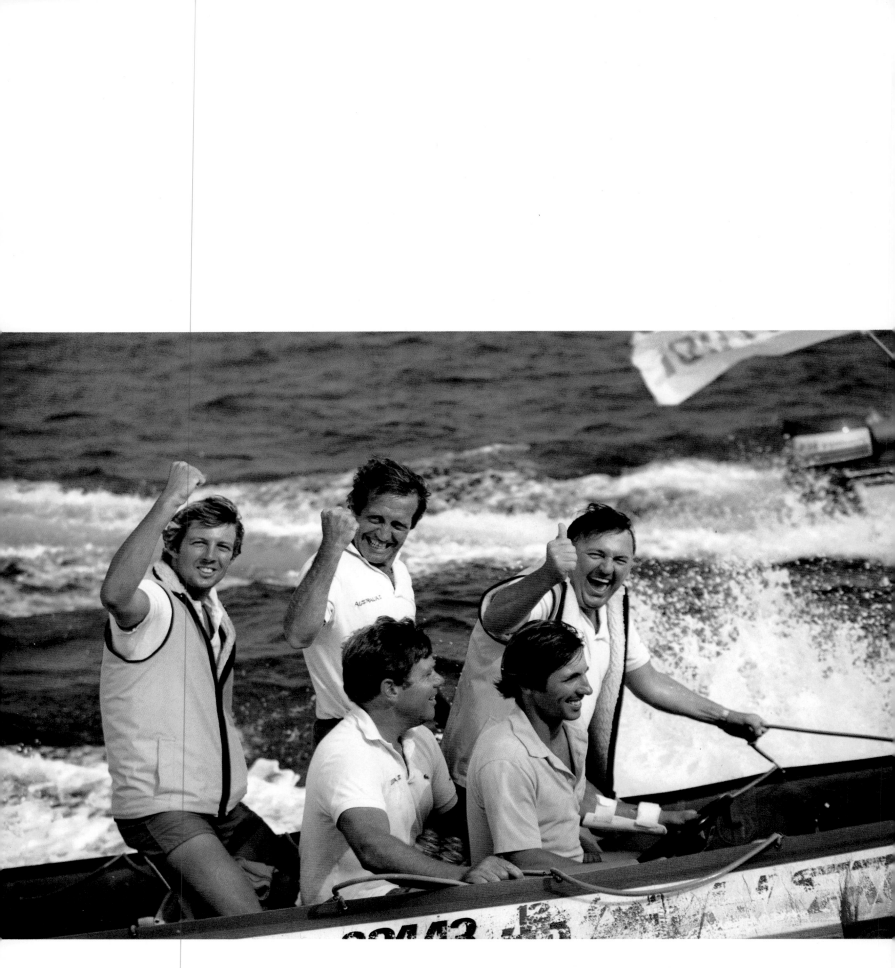

The entire Australian team beamed after the defeat of *Victory* '83. They had won the right to challenge the NYYC for the America's Cup — the vital first step on the road to ultimate victory. The occasion was marked by the unfurling of the Boxing Kangaroo flag, the brainchild of Executive Director Warren Jones. After seeing the 1980 British challenger *Lionheart's* flag, Winston the Bulldog, Jones decided the 1983 challenge needed a macho-looking mascot and the Boxing Kangaroo was the result.

PREVIOUS PAGE Newport welcomes *Australia II* after she wins the right to challenge.

Suitably attired for the day are *Australia II* crewmen Peter Costello (grinder: 193cm, 100kg), Phil Judge (*Black Swan* skipper: 178cm, 73kg), and John Longley (grinder: 196cm, 95kg).

PREVIOUS PAGE
Commonwealth vs England (crews) Cricket Match at
Beechwood, Mrs. Astor's summer house built in the best
tradition of the 1890's.

Spirits were also high in the stands, but decorum was maintained as somewhere in the crowd was Prince Andrew. The Commonwealth team (Australia and Canada) did their best, but HRH saw the British take the half-day match with several wickets in hand.

Besides cricket, the Australian crews' interest also strayed into hockey and
volleyball and they took part in several inter-crew matches involving the
British, Canadians and Italians. But their real interest was in sailing and with
four 18-footers present in Newport, spare time between the finals and the Cup
could be spent in maritime pursuits, usually led by 18-footer champion Rob
Brown.

As Newport geared up for the horde of America's Cup tourists, media people from around the world prepared for the trek to Rhode Island to witness what many thought would be another successful defence. But the Australian visitors, both press and otherwise, arrived with a quiet confidence that it would be at least a good fight.

Some Australian entrepreneurs had an eye on making some fast American dollars, while their American cousins were greatly underestimating the fibre of *Australia II*.

In true Great Gatsby style, the Preservation Society of Newport held the America's Cup Ball shortly before the Cup races began. Attended by 2000, the Ball was held at The Breakers, one of the most imposing Victorian mansions at Newport. The guests included Alan and Eileen Bond, Dennis Conner, John Fitzhardinge and his wife-to-be Judy Geoghegan.

THE RACES

AUSTRALIA II swept all before her during her long summer of campaigning. The British, the French, the Italians, the Canadians, and her two other Australian rivals, *Advance* from Sydney and *Challenge 12* from Melbourne, provided constant — though never entirely satisfactory — racing. The challenge elimination series, a veritable United Nations of 12-metre racing in which everyone demanded equal representation, often left *Australia II*, clearly the most superior yacht in Newport, with predictable processions rather than hard fought races. The Americans were meanwhile racing neck and neck, never more than a few feet apart, honing the exacting skills of close match racing. *Australia II* had the numbers on the board at the end of the elimination series but there remained an undercurrent of apprehension and doubt as she went out on that first day to meet the 'rusty red bucket' or the 'old Dutch barge' as the Australian crewmen dubbed *Liberty*.

The first race was a disaster for *Australia II* but it showed, for those with the eyes to see, that *Australia II* had better pointing ability and better boatspeed. She had the right stuff, the essential qualities that would take her on to a history-making win. No one, not even the most wildly imaginative Hollywood script-writer could have plotted a scenario such as that which unfolded on the Cup course. Tied at three-three with a sudden death sail-off in the seventh race was something not just unprecedented, but undreamed of in the 113-year history of Cup defence.

Although the infamous ITP's (Intensive Training Periods) of the early days
of physical training were over, the crew continued with an arduous exercise
schedule. Every morning, rain, fog or shine, the carpark at Founders' Hall
played host to the entire crew and their regimen of 138 push-ups plus a battery
of upper body exercises. To build stamina, everyone took to the backstreets of
Newport for several kilometres of roadwork. Much of *Australia II*'s success rests
with the excellent physical and mental condition of this crew and the absolute
dedication they had to winning.

Crewmembers wrestle with *Australia II*'s # 1 mast, a 28-metre length of specially extruded aluminium further customed by Ben Lexcen. This mast was so light that lead had to be added to the foot to bring the total weight up to the required 1000 pound minimum.

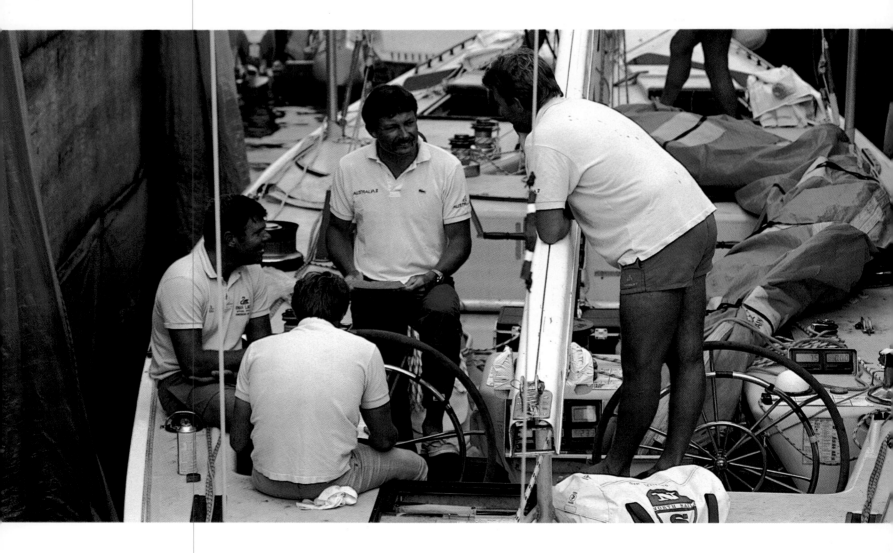

Lucas Bertrand was the crew's good luck charm — whenever he watched a race from *Black Swan*, the Australians won.

Hugh Treharne's children, Annaliese (in sailtrimmer's hatch) and Robbie visit their father at the office. On the deck behind Annaliese can be seen the sailtrimmer's two digital read-outs for boatspeed and windspeed. At right, maintenance chief and professional boatbuilder Ken Beashel finishes a model ocean racer for Lucas Bertrand.

RACE ONE

SEPTEMBER 14
LIBERTY d. AUSTRALIA II
BY ONE MINUTE 10 SECONDS

The first race was set down for Tuesday, September 13 but after months of anticipation it was to turn into a disappointing anticlimax. An enormous spectator fleet, variously estimated at between 1,500 and 2,000 vessels gathered in a great armada around the America's Cup buoy at 10 a.m. It was a glorious summer day, warm and sunny with a gentle north north easterly breeze, precisely the conditions *Australia II* wanted. In 13 years of covering America's Cup races I had never seen anything even remotely close to the size of this fleet. Yachts big and small had come from all over the world, bringing men and women who seemed to sense somehow that they would be eyewitnesses to history. The Coast Guard had 30 chase boats and half a dozen much larger vessels but they still were not enough to keep the mob under control. Perhaps it was just as well that the race was called off before it really began. That at least gave the spectators, many of whom I suspect had never before been to sea (let alone followed a yacht race), a sense of the discipline they would need if the races were to be sailed with fairness to both boats. But if the sea was alive with boats, the air was abuzz with helicopters and fixed wing aircraft. The choppers (I counted 60) whirred overhead in a great clockwise circle while above them, another bank of light aircraft went droning about in anti-clockwise loops. In the middle of them all,

The first race is postponed. The red and white postponement pennant can be seen in the background flying from *Black Knight's* signal mast.

like a great silver bullet, serene and unaffected by all this turbulent whizzing and buzzing, sat the majestic Goodyear blimp with its NYYC observer and a television camera crew.

Down behind the starting line stood the Coast Guard's glorious, white three-masted barque, *Eagle* and near her a sleek Navy destroyer flying from either side of her bridge the multi-coloured code flags that signalled Good Luck *Liberty*, Good Luck *Australia II*.

The NYYC's Race Committee vessel *Black Knight* took up her station ready for the 12.10pm start. At precisely 11.50am, the Race Committeemen all immaculate in Brenton red trousers, black jackets, white shirts and NYYC ties, hoisted the course signals indicating the bearing to the first mark would be 030 degrees. The nor'nor' easter was blowing at no more than eight knots. At noon the 10 minute warning gun boomed over Rhode Island Sound and the great racing yachts, one stark white and the other blood red, came in from either end of the line like jousting knights. The armchair admirals had all predicted furious turning and wheeling from the moment the boats met. Instead there was a tentative circling as each crew felt the other out. The circling became a little more intense before the five minute gun but then with just two minutes to the start the red and white striped postponement flag went up aboard *Black Knight*. The tension was broken and both boats retired, like boxers to their respective corners. The Race Committee had recorded a 40 degree shift to the east which meant if they had started on time it would have made the first leg into a reach instead of a beat to windward. The Coast Guard then had the monumental job of clearing the spectator boats away from the new course set as 090 degrees. The course signals went up once more at 1.50 pm. The countdown began at 2.00 and this time there was a lot more fire in the circling manoeuvres with *Australia II* clearly in command.

I had seen *Australia II* in action against lesser boats for three months but here at last was proof positive that she definitely had a significant edge over *Liberty*. She did not so much turn as pivot and this made her look like a dazzling butterfly at the start where the object of all this circling is to

120

dominate and control the rival boat. At 2.08pm a blue and white "A" flag was hoisted with the postponement pennant. The "A" signalled abandonment. This time the breeze had shifted 35 degrees to east south east and the Race Committee (together with Royal Perth Yacht Club's observer, John Fitzhardinge) decided that it was too late to try a third time. The enormous spectator fleet carried more than a few perplexed and disappointed passengers home to Newport that afternoon, but everyone later agreed that the NYYC had done the right thing.

The next day, September 14, dawned cold and overcast. A north easterly breeze (045 degrees) was blowing a true 18 knots and there was a slight chop on the grey-green sea. These were the conditions said to be ideal for *Liberty*, but *Australia II* surprised the Americans with her great stability and pointing ability. The start was fairly even. *Australia II* crossed the line three seconds ahead but with *Liberty* close by to windward. *Australia II* was able to lee bow the defender and force Conner to tack away for clear air. Conner and his tactician Tom Whidden stood on to the right hand side of the course on port tack but after nine minutes *Liberty* tacked to starboard. As the two boats crossed tacks for the first time it was clear the Australians were in front and a great war-whoop of joy went up from spectator boats festooned with green and gold ribbons. Bertrand immediately tacked on top of *Liberty* forcing Conner to tack back to port to keep his air clear. He stood on into a slight header, tacked onto right of way starboard and gained a narrow lead the next time they crossed. Both boats continued on starboard with the Australians on the inside of a lift that enabled them to cross ahead of *Liberty* again, tack and then cover her closely right to the starboard layline. *Australia II* rounded eight seconds ahead amid the howls and whoops and horns of support from the Australian spectators. It was the first time in modern America's Cup history that a foreign challenger had led an American defender around the first mark. It was in fact an omen of things to come. The Australians set a green and gold striped tri-radial kite and went racing off to the wing mark with *Liberty* hard on her heels under a red, white and blue striped chute.

Conner tried to eat into *Australia II*'s windward quarter, threatening to project *Liberty*'s wind shadow over the Australian boat. It didn't work, but in maintaining their position, the Australians were lulled into a false sense of security. They rounded the gybe mark 10 seconds ahead and when Conner tried the same tactic on the port gybe, they failed to respond quickly enough and Conner soon had the big red American boat riding up and through the Australian quarter wave. The Americans wore a beautiful flat-cut staysail beneath their spinnaker while the Australians had only just set theirs. Watching *Liberty* power right over the top of *Australia II* was one of the most awe inspiring sights of the entire Cup summer. After three months of watching often dreary processions around the race course we were now assured of a feast of truly magnificent match racing.

Liberty went around the leeward mark with a 26 second lead. Conner refused to allow himself to be drawn into a tacking duel and instead play the shifts beautifully while covering the Australians. The wind was shifting from five to 10 degrees and Conner said later that boats only several hundred yards apart were in different sailing conditions, the one on the inside of a lift going higher and looking faster. He also remarked about the difficulty in steering through the steep, choppy seas.

Liberty rounded the second windward mark 28 seconds ahead of *Australia II*. Her crew executed a perfect gybe-set, heading downhill on the more favored port gybe. Then the Australians, for the third time that day, astonished the Americans with a blistering turn of downwind speed.

Australia II came round the mark with a bear-away set and went off to the right under a beautiful white spinnaker. She gybed two minutes later but that short starboard hitch put her in a better breeze. Within 400 metres of the leeward mark she had closed to within two and a half lengths of the Americans and 70 metres to the right of them. With the mark to the right of them both, *Australia II* was nearer to it than *Liberty* and therefore almost on equal terms with the defender.

It was here that Conner and his crew executed one of the best and most daring moves of the entire summer. *Liberty*'s bowman, Scott Vogel was sent forward to prepare for a lightning gybe. Surprise was an absolutely vital element so Vogel slipped below and went to the forehatch unseen beneath the deck. When Conner gave the signal and swung the helm over, Vogel popped out like a jack-in-the-box and completed the dip-pole gybe in a twinkling. That left Bertrand with a couple of very quick decisions: he either gybed with Conner or crossed *Liberty*'s stern to try for an inside overlap at the mark. By gybing to starboard, Conner threw the burden of keeping clear back onto Bertrand. As the two boats converged on a collision course Bertrand put his helm hard down, aiming as he said later, to shoot across *Liberty*'s stern and then gybe.

It was a moment of tremendous stress for the steering gear. One of five under-deck pulleys linking the rudder to the wheel ripped out of its welded bracket and sent *Australia II* into a wild, out of control broach. Her spinnaker pole went sky high and sent the great green and gold kite thrashing and banging about overhead. Bertrand did a wonderful job in re-gaining control through the trim tab but by this time they were almost at the mark where the spinnaker had to come down and the headsail go up. The kite ended up in the water and the headsail and main were not sheeted home for more than half a minute after rounding the mark. By that time *Liberty* was a comfortable 35 seconds ahead. The Australians sailed on for 10 minutes steering only with their trim tab. Crewmen crawled into the cramped cavity aft to repair the damaged gear and the fact that *Australia II* managed to finish at all is a great tribute to their skill. *Liberty* won by one minute 10 seconds. That night Ken Beashel and the maintenance team strengthed all five steering pulleys and their brackets.

Conner and his crew were given a hero's welcome when they sailed home to Newport. Thousands came down to her dock to cheer and whistle encouragement as the American boat was hauled out of the water. Conner was pleased but cautious. "Wait," he said, "until we've got three more on the board."

While Warren Jones and Alan Bond discuss tactics on *Black Swan*, the
challenger and defender jockey for position before the start of the first race.
Australia II's amazing manoeuvrability and acceleration were immediately in
evidence. She was able to turn in a trice, well within her own length, leaving
Liberty wallowing in her wake.

On the first reaching leg, Conner tried to overtake Bertrand to windward, but *Liberty* could not match *Australia II*'s boatspeed and she fell back. However, on the second windward leg, Conner tried it again. *Australia II* did not cover the move in time and *Liberty* shot into the lead, but it was still very close.

PREVIOUS PAGE The challenger and defender head toward the starting line.

It was anyone's race until the last mark where Conner pushed Bertrand into making a violent manoeuvre in a choppy sea. The sudden pressure broke one of *Australia II's* steering blocks, causing her to momentarily career out of control. Although partial steering was soon restored, the margin between the boats was suddenly insurmountable and *Liberty* won handily. The record spectator fleet of 1500 boats, expecting a close race, were certainly not disappointed even though a last minute gear failure contributed to the American's win. They all headed back to Newport through the grey, cold of late afternoon to celebrate *Liberty's* first victory and the possibility of another brief Cup defence.

Dennis Conner had taken the first race, and, as was his habit, he sailed through the fleet to salute the NYYC and press boats. But Conner was cautious, he had witnessed *Australia II*'s speed at first hand and he knew mechanical failures could happen to *Liberty* as well. Similar thoughts were in the Australians' minds — they now knew their boat was faster and more manoeuvrable than the Americans and their problems could be readily repaired.

RACE TWO

SEPTEMBER 15
LIBERTY d. AUSTRALIA II
BY ONE MINUTE 33 SECONDS

The second race also went to *Liberty* but in truth it was over before it began. Six minutes before the start while *Australia II* was gybing in a violent gust (estimated to have been 24 knots true) she broke the uppermost of two specially hardened steel lugs used to secure the medium air mainsail headboard to its carrriage. The headboard swung down, pivoting around the lower lug and then the whole head of the sail tore along the lower edge of the headboard. The mainsail leech, with nothing to support it but a 5 mm diameter piece of Kevlar sagged down half a metre. That gave the main all the grace and drive of an empty potato sack. It says a lot for the energy and resourcefulness of the Australian crew, especially the great skill and dexterity of their mainsheet trimmer, Colin Beashel, that they not only went on with the race but very nearly won it.

The boom was down at decklevel but by raking the mast as far forward as it could go through hydraulic adjustment of the forestay, the Australians were able to get a bit of tension back into the leach and while the breeze held steady at 17 knots they were able to sail very fast indeed. Dennis Conner recalled that realisation as one of the most depressing parts of the entire Cup campaign. Even though all the odds seemed stacked against them, the Australians, through sheer sailing skill and dogged determination always managed to

hang in there. While the breeze was 030 degrees at the start, as the race wore on it faded to 13 knots and fell into the east north east at 055 degrees; this was to spell ultimate disaster for *Australia II*.

Liberty won the start by five seconds. *Australia II* was to windward at the gun but she soon tacked off with *Liberty* after her. Like a pathetic white bird with a crippled wing, *Australia II* lurched off on a long port tack, her main flogging and thundering but still driving. She was first into a heading shift and not long after tacking she crossed ahead of *Liberty*.

They split tacks again and when they came together seven minutes later *Australia II* was still in front. Conner initiated a savage tacking duel near the top mark in an attempt to aggravate *Australia II*'s mainsail problems but by this time the Australians had trimmed their rig so effectively that they survived 11 tacks in four minutes to hold *Liberty* out and carry her way past the starboard tack layline to the mark. It was an incredible comeback by the Australians. A 25 degree shift forced *Liberty* down into *Australia II*'s bad air. That meant the Americans were unable to lay the mark. Conner had to tack twice to clear it while the Australians scooted around 45 seconds ahead and romped away under the now familiar green and gold reaching kite.

Almost as soon as the spinnaker was up and drawing, Colin Beashel went aloft in a bosun's chair. Beashel deserves special mention because his extraordinary natural skills (he is a member of Sydney's legendary sailing Beashels) kept Australian hopes alive. Working alone at the masthead, 28 metres above the water, he spent 18 minutes on the two reaching legs securing the head of the main to the masthead carriage with lashing rove through a hole he punched in the headboard with a spike. But *Liberty* narrowed the gap to 31 seconds at the gybe mark and 21 seconds at the leeward mark.

The easing breeze meant an end to Australian hopes and *Liberty* relentlessly pulled them back on the fourth leg. Conner caught them half way

up that 4.5 mile leg. Toward the end of the fourth leg Conner dropped what the Americans call a "slam-dunk" manoeuvre on the Australians. As he crossed in front, he tacked immediately upwind to bring the Australians directly under his wind shadow. A red protest flag immediately appeared on *Australia II*. Bertrand alleged the American tactic had forced him to alter course to avoid a collision. The international jury disallowed the protest, heard the following day. It maintained that *Australia II* would have missed *Liberty* if Bertrand had held his course.

Liberty came around the fourth mark 48 seconds in front. The Australians pulled them back to 31 seconds after the downhill run under spinnaker but on the final beat to the finish their crippled mainsail was more and more obvious in the light air. The breeze had swung 25 degrees and a new course was signalled by the race committee boat *Black Knight*. As the breeze faded it backed and veered in a series of 20 degree shifts. Under those circumstances Bertrand and Treharne felt they had nothing to lose by going off in search of a breeze. They split tacks in a last bold gamble to find a wind shift to the left. They never found it and *Liberty* came home an easy winner by one minute 33 seconds.

With the score now 2-0, the Australian faced the grim prospect of going the way of every other Cup challenger. I remember Warren Jones, grim faced in his dockside office as he said: "We've got to win this next one or we're done for. It's bad enough being two-nil but coming back from three-nil would be beyond even Lazarus." It was a side of Jones that the *Australia II* crew rarely, if ever, saw. At the crew house he was always Mr Positive, Jones had already chalked the victory onto his planning board. The space under September 24 (his birthday) said "Win the Cup". He was only two days out.

Although there was a dispute over who called the following lay day, the international jury decided it was the Australians and both boats spent the day in Newport while their sailmakers worked to repair some sails and refine others.

Unfortunately, luck was not with the Australians once again. Shortly before the start, the upper lug on the mainsail headboard fractured in a sudden gust of wind, the sail went slack and the aft end of the boom dropped into *Australia II's* cockpit. The main flapped ineffectually as the crew frantically adjusted the mast as far forward as the hydraulic forestay controls could bend it. Eventually there was enough tension in the sail for it to draw, but it could not be sheeted hard and *Australia II* started the race pointing poorly.

With her mast raked noticibly forward, her headboard down from the masthead by some 20cm and her boom barely clearing the deck, *Australia II* is not the perfect picture of a modern Twelve. However, even though she cannot point as high as *Liberty* (for the first time in the series), she still has boatspeed in the brisk wind and runs neck and neck with the defender.

As long as the wind held, *Australia II* stayed with *Liberty*. They are followed around the course by the 'privilege fleet', an assortment of craft from the inner circle of the NYYC, RPYC and other institutions of clout, that were issued with 'privilege pennants'. These red and yellow flags were individually numbered with the boat's place in the fleet, so the number 20 boat had to stay behind or next to the number 19 boat and so forth.

The International Jury boat, at left between the yachts, follows the race closely. With video cameras and the jury itself on board, they can monitor any close encounters first hand and in case of a protest bring down a fair decision. Coming to the wing mark, above, *Australia II* still leads *Liberty*.

Mainsheet trimmer Colin Beashel, 24, spent most of the two reaching legs suspended in a bosun's chair 27 metres above the deck of *Australia II* securing the damaged headboard. While clinging precariously to the masthead, he punched a hold in the aluminium reinforced headboard with a marlinespike then threaded kevlar ribbon through the hole, around the masthead and back again. It was an extraordinary act of bravery and seamanship and the reinforcement saved the #1 mainsail from serious damage.

Australia II manages to retain her slight lead despite the damaged mainsail.
Colin Beashel's repairs allowed the main to be sheeted in somewhat tighter,
but it was still far from efficient. Toward the end of the race the wind began to
lighten and this was disastrous for the Australians. After fighting so hard with a
crippled boat, the light winds made sail efficiency paramount and the
Americans, in a very close manoevre, slipped in front of the challengers and
went on to win.

Another equipment failure and another great disappointment for the Australians. It was the first time in 15 months of sailing that a headboard tang had broken. John Longley remembers . . . "During the second windward leg of the race *Australia II* on port tack bore away to clear *Liberty's* stern. Just as she was about to do so, Conner immediately tacked and Bertrand in surprise tacked to try and clear *Liberty's* stern. At this point, we raised our protest flag (above), claiming that *Liberty* had tacked too close." Later in the protest *Australia II* bowman Damian Fewster claimed that the boats were less than two feet apart. The jury found that the distance was four feet and felt that was sufficient room for a 23-tonne yacht moving at 8 knots. John recalls that Bertrand was amazed that the boats did not actually collide. The jury found there was sufficient room for manoeuvring, the protest was not allowed and the score stood at 2-0.

RACE THREE

SEPTEMBER 17 (ABANDONED)
RE-RUN SEPTEMBER 18
AUSTRALIA II d. LIBERTY
BY 3 MINUTES 14 SECONDS

Over 1,500 boats turned out on Saturday, September 17 to see if *Australia II* could get it all together. She did but the clock beat her. The race started in a perfect 10 knot south-easterly and Bertrand, having won the start in decisive fashion, went on to round the first mark first for the third successive time, leading *Liberty* by one minute 15 seconds. The heavier *Liberty* was simply no match for the lighter Australian boat and at the end of the two reaching legs she was one minute 58 seconds astern. The margin was one minute 46 seconds at the second windward mark and a staggering five minutes 57 seconds behind at the end of the square run. That was the largest single gap any Cup challenger had ever opened over an American defender. The Australians sailed a first class race but deep and unavoidable calm patches on the last three legs of the course deprived them of a certain win. Half way up the last leg, with *Liberty* more than half a mile astern, a south westerly breeze piped up and sent Australian hopes soaring until someone calculated that she would have to sail that last leg at an average of 30 knots to win. *Australia II* was fast but not quite that fast. With one and a half miles to the line the race committee raised the dreaded "A" flag to signal race abandoned. The score remained two-nil

in favour of the defender.

After yet another delay, the third race re-match got under way on Sunday September 18 in a true south westerly wind (225 degrees) of seven knots. This was to be *Australia II*'s day, a convincing step along the comeback trail.

These were, once again, perfect conditions for *Australia II* and Conner seemed reluctant to tangle with Bertrand in the pre-start manoeuvres. Conner left Bertrand alone and went for the Committee Boat end of the line. Although *Liberty* is credited with an eight second advantage at the gun, the gap between the boats was in fact more even. *Australia II* was moving much faster than the defender because Conner had to luff almost head-to-wind to clear the long anchor line set from the Race Committee boat.

The Australian weathermen correctly predicted that the left hand side of the track would be favoured early in the race as the young south-west breeze filled in, matured then followed the traditional swing to the right. Both boats stood-on on port tack for 22 minutes in an extraordinary "drag race", a test of pure straight line speed. *Australia II* had the edge, sailing a steady two degrees higher and steadily climbing out to windward.

When *Liberty* eventually tacked onto star-board, *Australia II* crossed ahead with a five boat-length advantage. The Americans tossed seven tacks at the Australians to try to break free of their covering grip but *Australia II* was easily able to stay in control by virtue of her speed through tacks and her rapid acceleration out of them. At the first mark she was one minute 14 seconds ahead.

Liberty closed to within 52 seconds at the wing mark and, capitalising on a tighter second reaching leg she made good use of an almost transparent Mylar staysail to gain a further 10 seconds.

That 42 second edge at the leeward mark enabled the Australians to clamp a very effective cover on the Americans. There was a real sense of desperation about the American tactics on the second windward leg. Conner tried everything; straight-line sailing for speed, quick tacking, headsail changes and yet nothing seemed to make the slightest impression on the Australian flying machine. *Australia II* went away to a one minute 15 second lead at the end of the fourth leg and stretched that to two minutes 47 seconds at the end of the square run. On the last leg she showed tremendous power and pointing ability in the 10 knot breeze to win by three minutes 14 seconds. It was the ninth win by a challenger in 103 years, but it was the biggest margin since 12-metre yachts began to race for the Cup in 1958.

Dennis Conner called for a lay day. *Liberty* clearly needed a real breeze to match the Australians. Gary Jobson, tactician aboard *Defender* and my co-broadcaster of the series for the ABC gave Conner, his old rival, full marks for trying.

"Conner and his crew did everything perfectly," he said. "They tried to draw Bertrand into mistakes in tacking duels (29 tacks on the second beat), they tried to attack him on the reaches and they gybed seven times to what could have been favourable wind slants on the run. They were just outclassed by boatspeed. In the conditions today *Australia II* is truly 'Superboat'."

Alan Bond never referred to any crew member as back-up or reserve. This set a precedent in that everyone involved in the challenge was an equal member of the team and this contributed immensely to the unity of the group. In addition, several of the crew members are related — mainsail trimmer and headboard repairer Col Beashel is the son of maintenance chief Ken, and sailtrimmer Ken Judge, in the sail storage container above, is the brother of *Black Swan* skipper Phil.

Even though the first attempt at a third race ended with
the allowed time running out, it was a vindication for
the Australians. The two consecutive defeats were
discouraging even to a group as well trained as this crew
and this time they had beaten *Liberty* convincingly. So
as the time ran out on the last leg with *Australia II* some
half mile ahead of *Liberty,* the crew recorded the event,
above, with *Liberty* present only as a sail on the horizon.

Winning the re-run of the third race quickly restored confidences. Now they knew for sure *Liberty* could be beaten. But there was still a long way to go and there was very little room for mistakes. *Australia II* had proved herself when it really counted by beating *Liberty* to every mark and finishing with a three minute, 14 second advantage, the greatest winning margin by a challenger since Twelves have contended the Cup.

With her first victory chalked on the board, *Australia II* heads up Narragansett Bay past Castle Hill and into Newport Harbour. For the first time it was the Australians' turn to celebrate.

Perched right on the waterfront, perennially popular Christie's Restaurant is one of Newport's traditions. During the summer it gradually became an Australian bar, due no doubt in part to its proximity to the Australian syndicate headquarters across the street at Newport Offshore. The *Australia II* crew, however, was rarely there due to the rigour of their training.

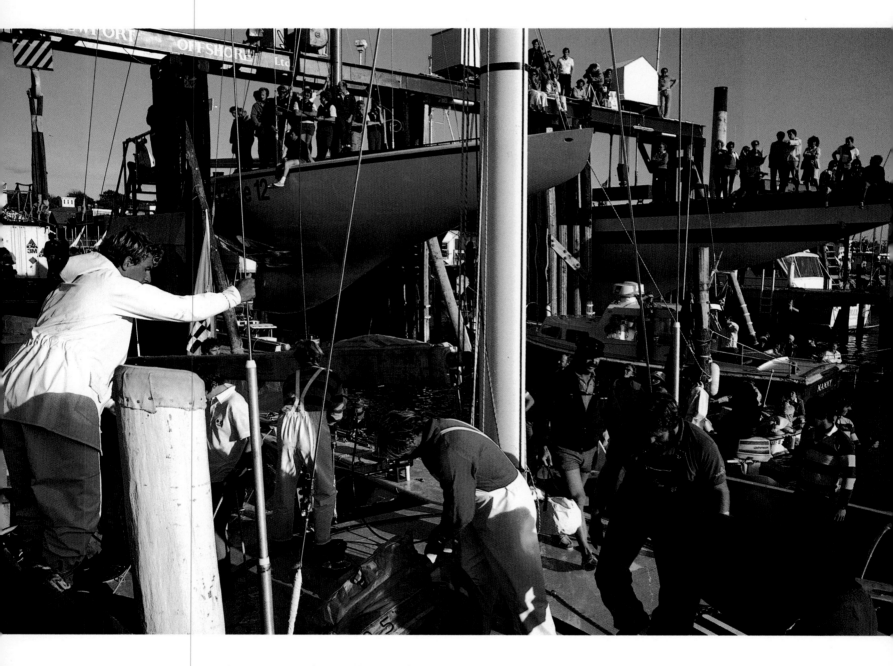

After a day's sailing, all *Australia II*'s sails were unloaded and stored in the 20-foot container used as the sail locker. They were examined thoroughly and any damage repaired before sailing the next day.

Both John Fitzhardinge and Ben Lexcen put in long working days at Newport. Besides his duties as rigger, 'Fitzy' was the syndicate representative on *Black Knight* and he always sailed with them immaculate in dark blazer, white shirt and black tie. Ben, on the other hand, had the keel controversy behind him and liked nothing better than helping with the day to day maintenance.

Dousing *Australia II*'s green and gold spinnaker, grinder Peter Costello, an Army major, gets some experience on the foredeck while champion oarsman and grinder Brian Richardson, bottom right, watches intently.

Mastman and America's Cup veteran Phil Smidmore,
on left, confers with chase-boat skipper Mark Reid.

The crew had little spare time during the Cup series. There was always the opportunity to practice more or test sails, and most crewmen took it. As *Australia II* works to weather, sailtrimmer and tailer Rob Brown, left, works with grinder Will Baillieu sharpening their combined talents.

Navigator and computer expert Grant Simmer, above, was one of *Australia II*'s 'afterguard'. This group of three consists of the helmsman (Bertrand), the tactician (Treharne) and the navigator. During a race, they are constantly conferring on the progress of the race, combining their skills of boat handling, tactics and interpretation of computer data to either keep the yacht in the lead or catch the opposition.

RACE FOUR

SEPTEMBER 20
LIBERTY d. AUSTRALIA II
BY 43 SECONDS

Race four started in magnificent sunny conditions typical of Newport in the late summer. The horizon was veiled with a light misty haze and the breeze was at west south west (235 degrees) and 10 knots for the start. *Liberty* won the start by six seconds and with it the race. In the early stages of the pre-start manoeuvres Bertrand kept Conner bobbing and weaving as they circled but with a minute to go he seemed to misjudge his position in relation to the line. He had planned to cross on starboard tack near its right hand end, timing his approach so that Conner who was on port, would have to dip behind to observe the right of way port-starboard rule. *Australia II* was sitting in a stalled head to head situation with *Liberty* with just three and a half minutes to go when she broke off and appeared to sail too far away from the line to duck back in time. With about 60 seconds to the gun *Australia II* was on starboard and close reaching for the committee boat end of the line while *Liberty* on port tack headed for the Committee boat. Conner showed the great judgemental skill and icy calm that have made him a legendary figure in international yachting when he held his course and crossed no more than 10 or perhaps 15 feet in front of *Australia II* to win the start by six seconds. Bertrand conceded later that he misjudged the start. "It was," he said, "purely a judgmental error on my part."

Liberty stood on to the right of the upwind leg for three minutes, deliberately ignoring *Australia II*'s uncovered starboard tack course to the left, but the Americans knew what they were doing. The defender got all the lifts that traditionally favour the right hand track in a south westerly wind while the Australians, who stuck resolutely to the left got all the knocks.

When they came together *Liberty* had shot into a commanding lead. At the first mark the Americans were 36 seconds ahead.

Liberty gained 12 seconds on the first reaching leg and the margin remained 48 seconds at the leeward mark. Conner and Whidden pretty much ignored traditional match race tactics that demand a leading boat stay between its opponent and the mark and went instead in search of every slant they could find. The Australians were left with no option but follow on. They did and *Liberty* led them around the second windward mark by 46 seconds.

Australia II had an established reputation as a downhill flier but she was too far behind in these conditions to do anything more than take 11 seconds out of the Americans. She rounded 35 seconds astern but with the breeze freshening to 15 knots for the final beat and the Americans capitalising on every wind shift, *Liberty* was able to walk away to a comfortable 43 seconds win.

As *Australia II* backed into her berth at Newport Offshore, a weary John Bertrand looked up and told me: "I'll never endure a humiliation like that again." Bertrand was as good as his word. At 3-1 down, *Australia II* was about to earn its place in history.

Liberty led *Australia II* convincingly around the course with the Australians never seriously threatening. "They beat us fair and square" remarked John Longley. With the score now 3-1 and the Australians' backs tight against the wall, Alan Bond invoked the hallowed names of Gallipoli and Anzac and looked unflinchingly ahead at three straight Australian victories.

RACE FIVE

SEPTEMBER 21
AUSTRALIA II d. LIBERTY
BY ONE MINUTE 47 SECONDS

After so many mechanical faults plagueing the Australians in the early races, there were those (Australian supporters) who thought it only fit and proper that the Americans should have a few as well. An hour before the fifth race started, while *Liberty* was tuning up with her trial horse *Freedom*, she bent the ³/₄ inch diameter stainless steel ram which tensions the aluminium jumper struts. The struts collapsed and with them went effective control of the upper third of the American mast and through it, control of the upper part of the powerful mainsail.

Liberty at first sought permission from the race committee to have a replacement flown out by helicopter, but when this request was turned down, its fastest support boat, the 40 knot skiff *Rhonda*, dashed the 11 miles to Castle Hill, at the entrance to Narragansett Bay, where it picked up the spare jumpers from an inflatable runabout.

In the meantime *Liberty*'s bowman Scott Vogel and Tom Rich her pitman went aloft to dismantle the collapsed jumpers. Vogel and Rich deserve the highest praise for an extraordinary display of great courage and seamanship. They worked on the swaying mast despite a nasty, lumpy sea that pitched them about and left them badly bruised. The replacement was passed to *Liberty* and the work completed just two minutes before the 10 minute warning gun sounded. Vogel

and Rich spent 50 minutes up the mast and returned to the deck exhausted and clearly in no condition to race. But they did. As part of the three man foredeck gang, they had to immediately get on with the task of setting the headsail as the yachts prepared to come together for the vital pre-start manoeuvres.

The breeze was west south westerly (190 degrees) with a lumpy, confused sea.

Australia II leapt to attack the disadvantaged Americans, but Conner soon threw them off by wheeling around behind an enormous Coast Guard ship. Bertrand and his afterguard misjudged the start by something under a metre and although they pushed *Liberty* over the line early, the Americans were able to duck back and successfully re-cross while the Australians sat almost motionless in the water on the wrong side of the line. *Liberty* was off and running on port tack while *Australia II* was forced to ease away, run back behind the line, gybe and set out in pursuit fully 37 seconds astern. It was by far the worst start of the entire series and it demonstrated clearly just how fine a line there is between a brilliant manoeuvre and one that brings forth the scorn of all the armchair admirals. I must confess, I for one thought the Australian game was up as

I looked at the distance between the two boats. But as it turned out, Conner needed all that and more.

Three or four minutes later, *Liberty*'s port jumper strut gave way again. The repair work had not been completely effective because the hydraulic cylinder had been damaged and the steel rod remained fully extended.

Without proper tension on the jumpers, *Liberty*'s mast sagged off badly whenever she sailed on port tack. *Liberty* was still sailing as fast but lower on port. It was a severe handicap, and yet Conner held onto port tack because he expected the shifts would clock right. They didn't. *Australia II* tacked away from *Liberty* onto starboard and made for the middle of the course. Conner stayed on port for five minutes before he realised how grave an error he had made. *Australia II* sailed into a five degree header and when she tacked back and the boats came together, they were dead even. *Australia II* tacked back to starboard on *Liberty*'s lee bow.

After 10 very quick tacks in just five minutes, *Australia II* had regained her lead. There was no 12-metre yacht in the world that could tack and accelerate as quickly as *Australia II*. The Australians timed their tacks to dump the maximum amount of dirty or disturbed air on the American sails whenever they caught *Liberty* on starboard tack. They gave her free air on port tack and thereby encouraged Conner to go right. The Australians, at all costs, wanted to protect their advantage on the left.

Australia II rounded the top mark 23 seconds ahead and held precisely the same margin at the wing mark. *Liberty* pegged them back to 18 seconds by the leeward mark, but pointing higher and accelerating much faster out of tacks, *Australia II* shot ahead to round the fourth mark a comfortable one minute 11 seconds ahead.

The Americans set a very big spinnaker for the square run and it helped pull them up to within 52 seconds of the Australians at the bottom mark. But that margin was more than enough for *Australia II*, and with Bertrand applying only a loose cover, they raced away to a convincing one minute 47 second win. It was the first time a 12-metre challenger had won two races in a Cup series. *Gretel II* won two in 1970 but was disqualified by what was then the NYYC's own protest committee.

The score stood at 3-2. Bertrand had the satisfaction of erasing some of the fourth race humiliation he spoke so passionately about. But he must go on winning and the odds, the overwhelming odds and the crushing weight of history, were against him. Bertrand, in typical fashion, seemed not the least bit phased. "One day at a time," he used to say, "One day at a time."

Liberty was stiffer with the broken jumper struts and her crew hiked out as she drove to windward. This practice is unusual in modern 12-metre yachts although it was standard procedure fifteen years ago. At left, the starboard trimmer's gaze is firmly fixed on the luff as he calls the trim. Headsail trim was absolutely critical with the crippled mast.

As their bows slice through the water, *Australia II* and *Liberty* show why Twelves are called the ultimate racing yacht. These 23-tonnes speedsters are not stopped by waves, they power straight through leaving their crews hanging on for dear life as green water sweeps across the deck.

Balloons, intended to mark *Liberty*'s America's Cup victory, forlornly mark her second defeat. Losing by mechanical fault was a situation *Australia II* knew all too well, but the Australian boat was really in the groove now and the conjecture around Newport said she was a winner with or without *Liberty*'s mast failure. The Australians had the first win of their hat-trick and they too felt their boat had hit its stride and could turn the tables on the Americans.

PREVIOUS PAGE
Australia II begins the second leg comfortably ahead of *Liberty*.

PREVIOUS PAGE NYYC Committee members aboard
Black Knight line the port rail to acknowledge
Australia II's victory in the 5th race.
200

Exuberance and liquid refreshment abound after
Australia's second win. While delighted spectators give
their congratulations to the *Australia II* runabout, other
supporters raise the flag in salute while weaving
precariously through part of the Newport fleet. Backing
into their berth at Newport Offshore, Alan Bond, at
right, and the crew savour a second moment of victory

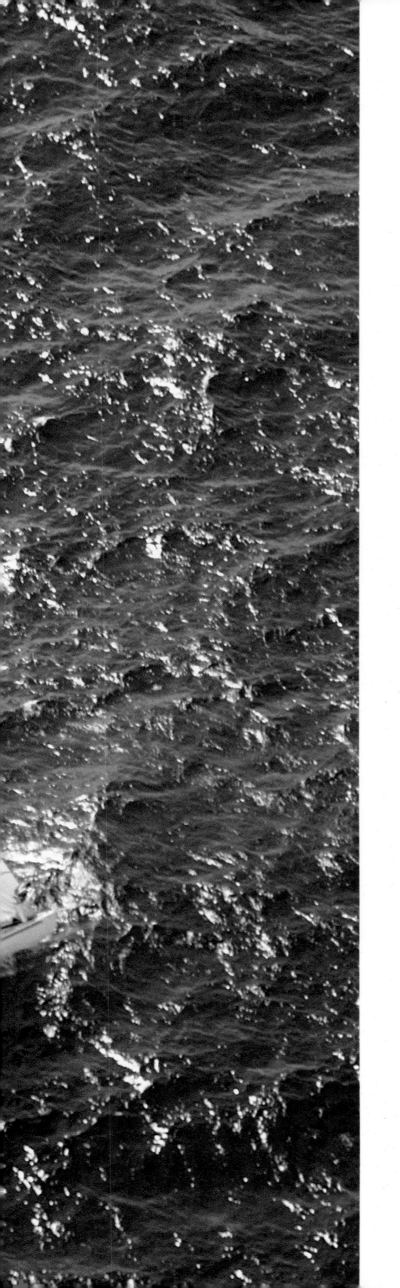

RACE SIX

SEPTEMBER 22
AUSTRALIA II d. LIBERTY
BY THREE MINUTES 25 SECONDS

Thursday, September 22, was an historic day for *Australia II* and for America's Cup competition. It was the day when she became the first challenger in the 113 year history of the event to square a match three-all and her winning margin of three minutes and 25 seconds was the widest ever recorded by a 12-metre challenger.

The wind at the start was a cool 12 knot north north-westerly (340 degrees) that would later back to the west (forcing two course changes for the second and final beats) and freshen to between 16 and 19 knots.

For the third successive race, Bertrand misjudged his start. After approaching it too early on starboard tack, he had to gybe, circle and cross behind *Liberty* on port, seven seconds late at the line. *Liberty* tacked to port and was nicely placed on the inside of a lift that helped her cross *Australia II*.

The Australians tacked to starboard and went way off to the left hand side of the course. The Americans followed them four minutes after the start.

After 14 minutes, *Australia II* tacked onto port. Conner tacked in front of them, ahead by two boat lengths. That forced the Australians to tack away and into a header. Conner was content to hang on to his port tack lift and he ignored *Australia II*. When Bertrand tacked back onto

port, he found himself on *Liberty*'s quarter.

But now it was the Australian's turn to benefit from the patchy breeze. While *Liberty* sailed into a lull and was forced to bear away, *Australia II* found herself in a fresher patch and began to lift out and up in a dramatic comeback. After 10 minutes, *Liberty* found a light header and tacked to starboard, staggering back towards the Australians.

Australia II then came back at Liberty and dumped so much dirty air on the Americans that Conner was forced to tack away onto port. That manoeuvre put *Australia II* into an extraordinary port tack lift. She tacked into it and lifted almost straight to the windward mark. *Liberty* was left a long way to leeward in much lighter air.

The breeze had dropped to no more than five knots at the mark and *Australia II* came round with a whopping lead of two minutes 29 seconds.

The Australians lost only one second on the first reach as they swept around the wing mark with a beautifully executed gybe in which they simultaneously peeled to a running spinnaker for the third leg which had become a run. She came round the bottom mark three minutes 46 seconds ahead. The race committee signalled a course change to 295 degrees for the second windward leg, but the breeze continued to freshen and swing into the south west. *Australia II* clamped a very effective cover on *Liberty* all the way up the second beat, effectively blocking any prospect for Conner's recovery. She rounded three minutes

206

22 seconds ahead.

It was an indication of just how desperate and how frustrated Conner had become when *Liberty* quite deliberately came at *Australia II* close hauled on starboard tack as the Australians came down the fifth leg under spinnaker. It was all quite within the racing rules; a boat on a free leg of the course (*Australia II*) must give way to a boat close hauled (*Liberty*) but there were those, including Alan Bond, who found it a bit beyond the pale that the Americans set out to force a foul which could have disqualified *Australia II*.

Bertrand saw what was happening and hardened up so that he cleared *Liberty*'s bow by two boatlengths.

Australia II came round the leeward mark four minutes eight seconds ahead and covered easily on the last leg to finish three minutes 25 seconds in front.

The gun from the committee boat signalled a tremendous outpouring of support for *Australia II*. Americans in their thousands came to stand 12 deep around the *Australia II* dock, cheering, stamping and whistling their hopes that after 21 years of trying, the Australians might be on the brink of beating the NYYC. Alan Bond signalled a lay day to give his crew a chance to rest up for what the whole world now confidently expected would be the yacht race of the century.

But there were to be a few more disappointments before that magic moment arrived.

Looking unbeatably powerful, *Liberty* thunders along on starboard tack. But she was no match for *Australia II* in either pointing ability or boat speed.

Sporting her revolutionary tri-radial headsail and her medium air mainsail, *Australia II* romps home a clear winner in the 6th race.

FOLLOWING PAGE Instead of the usual tow, *Australia II* sails back to Newport in triumph.

The Australians had their third win, the Cup was tied and an armada of enthusiastic supporters surrounded *Australia II*. Everyone loves a winner and with spirits high there were bumps galore between boats as they jostled for position next to the Australians. Soon this great raft of boats began the procession back to Newport.

Five thousand Australians were in Newport for the America's Cup races. All of them, plus thousands of other visitors, turned up to welcome the Australian boat back to her dock. Newport Offshore swarmed with well-wishers and boxing kangaroo flags were everywhere. A giant Australian flag flew from *Challenge 12's* mast. This was the first time in the history of the Cup that a challenger and defender were tied at 3-3.

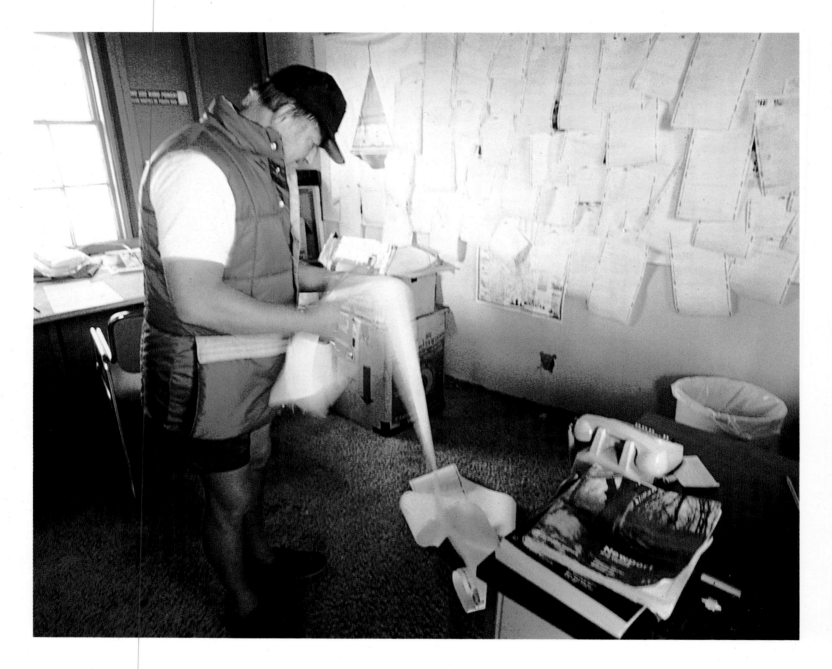

Alan Bond takes time to read some telexes in *Australia II*'s Newport
headquarters. The office was innundated with tens of thousands of messages of
support from Australia and around the world and the walls ended up papered
with them like the inside of a drover's hut.

While Bruce Stannard called the races from Newport, the ABC had its own experts in their Sydney studios. Ocean racing veteran Peter Shipway seems amused by *Dame Pattie* designer Warwick Hood's anguish when the first attempt at a 7th and deciding race was abandoned. ABC anchorman Alan Marks, at right, looks on sympathetically.

RACE SEVEN

SEPTEMBER 24
FIRST ATTEMPT ABANDONED
SEPTEMBER 26
AUSTRALIA II d. LIBERTY
BY 41 SECONDS

Alan Bond's 'rest' for the crew was well inten-
tioned, but never really materialised. After a
morning of thorough checking, Bertrand took
Australia II out to match wits in pre-start manoeuvres with Harold Cudmore, the Irish match
racing afficiandado who had dropped out of the
Victory '83 syndicate following a disagreement
with Peter de Savary.

There was no real rest for the American crew,
either. Most of them spent the day up at the Cove
Haven Marina at Barrington, about 30 km from
Newport, where *Liberty* was remeasured after
920 lbs of lead were removed from her ballast
package Conner was determined to do whatever
he could to stave off the Australian threat.
Putting *Liberty* into her "light air mode" very
nearly did the trick. It allowed *Liberty* to increase
the size of her mainsail by about 22 sq ft. During
the trials, Conner had used *Liberty*'s multiple rat-
ing certificates to great advantage over the other
defence candidates, *Defender* and *Courageous*.
They were not told the NYYC's America's Cup
committee had given Conner special permission
to use multiple ratings. They allowed *Liberty* to
have three different certificates, one for each
"mode", light, medium and heavy air. But in the
end it was thought that all this chopping and

changing might have, in some ways, acted against *Liberty*'s best interests. On September 24, after two abandoned attempts to start the seventh race, Conner announced that he would change *Liberty*'s ballast package again. Once again the crew had to endure the tedius six hour ritual of towing to Barrington, hauling out and plumbing the boat dead vertical, only to be told at the last minute the latest weather forecast meant they would be staying in their light weather configuration after all.

There was another aborted start on Monday, September 26 when the eight to 10 knot south south westerly wind shifted and officials called a halt at 12.08 p.m. after eight minutes of manoeuvring. Then at 1.05 p.m. in a breeze of 205 degrees, the yacht race of the century finally got under way. It began with caution. The boats circled warily and sometimes drove in and feinted. Those who had expected blood and guts were disappointed; Dennis Conner knew only too well the extraordinary turning ability of this Australian boat and he was not about to do anything to prevent his pulling this series out of the fire.

Liberty appeared a lot more lively with so much lead out. With two minutes to the gun, both boats approached the line on starboard; *Liberty* ready to go off to Conner's favourite right hand side of the course and Bertrand happy to go to the left. *Liberty* tacked away and started on port. She crossed the line eight seconds ahead of *Australia II* and set out immediately looking for the shifts that would help her compensate for

Australia II's phenomenal light air ability.

But it was *Australia II* that found them on the left, and when the boats converged 18 minutes after the gun, she was a clear two lengths in front. Two minutes later *Liberty* tacked onto starboard. *Australia II* crossed on port, three or four boat-lengths ahead, then tacked onto starboard covering on *Liberty*'s air. That forced Conner to tack away onto port.

Australia II came about on port, then *Liberty* immediately tossed back to starboard. The Australians held on for four minutes and allowed Conner to split tacks and go a long way to the left. John Bertrand was severely criticised by the media for his failure to cover, but as he explained later, he did not have sufficient wind pressure to quickly tack and effectively cover *Liberty*. And besides, he was convinced the next shift would come from the right.

Instead, it was a header from the left that knocked *Australia II* down toward *Liberty*'s line. The next time they crossed, they were dead even. *Liberty* tacked on *Australia II*'s lee bow and forced Bertrand onto port to clear his air. The Australians had lost the advantage and now the Americans clamped a close cover on them. It was a tactical gain that seemed likely to keep the Cup safely on its pedestal in the NYYC.

Liberty came around the first mark 29 seconds ahead amid wild cheering and horn blasting from the enormous spectator fleet, again estimated at about 1500. The Americans picked up 16 seconds to lead by 45 seconds at the gybe mark. A 10 degree shift had converted this first broad reach into a very tight one, but that made the second leg a square run, a point of sailing in which *Australia II* was clearly superior. *Black Knight* signalled the new course, 195 degrees, and *Australia II* closed to within 23 seconds of *Liberty* at the bottom mark.

Conner sailed a magnificent second windward leg. At no stage did he allow Bertrand to escape from his cover, and at the end of the second beat, *Liberty*, giving by far the best light air account of herself ever, had managed to stretch the gap to 57 seconds. It looked to many spectators as if the boat race was all over. But *Australia II*'s incredible down-wind speed over *Liberty* was to prove her trump card.

Soon after she rounded the top mark, *Liberty*

gybed to port and sailed back toward the centre of the course to escape the so called "fence" effect of the spectator fleet, which not only blocked the breeze, but threw up disturbed water as well. The Australians went precisely the opposite way after a beautiful bear-away spinnaker set. But instead of sailing into spectator slop, the Australians found themselves in fresh air.

Liberty, unlike most conventional 12-metres, is comparatively slow when she runs dead square. So Conner made five gybes, angling the breeze across his stern as much as possible to increase his boat's speed and use whatever shifts there were to his advantage. *Australia II*, which was almost as fast running dead square as *Liberty* on a quartering run, simply sailed "deeper", at smaller angles to the mark, and therefore had less distance to cover. Ben Lexcen believes *Australia II* gained so dramatically on this leg because she had a much better shape in the water, she had at least a two and a half tonne weight advantage over *Liberty*, and of the greatest significance, she had smaller, more efficient spinnakers which were better trimmed than those aboard the American boat.

Two thirds of the way to the bottom mark, *Australia II* had run *Liberty* down, and at the end of the leg she was 21 seconds ahead. It was an incredible moment, watching that big white kite with its green and gold bars slide on past *Liberty*'s red, white and blue. Right across Australia, millions of bleary eyed fanatics who had stayed up all night to watch the spectacle on television and listen on radio, sensed they were all part of history in the making. But there was still another agonising 4.5 miles to go, and Dennis Conner showed he would fight every inch of the way. He launched a desperate and sustained tacking duel — the likes of which are rarely seen in big boat match racing. Forty-seven times he tossed *Liberty* about and forty-seven times he was met by a grim Australian defence. Conner twice tried the false tack, dummying to tack and then falling back to his original heading, while *Australia II* was left hung-up head-to-wind and more committed to completing her tack. It went on for two minutes short of an hour. This was the supreme test of the crews fitness. All those mornings of relentless jogging and press-ups and exercises, all the stamina and will power that had been wrought over two and in some cases three years, was now being called upon. Neither crew was found wanting.

In one last desperate attempt to outfox the Australians, Conner lured them to the very edge of the spectator fleet on the starboard side of the layline in the hope they might become tangled up in all the confused sea and air from that vast armada of vessels. But Bertrand kept his cool and when he was certain he could make the finish line, he turned and left Conner sailing away from the mark. All the Americans could do was turn and follow in his wake. As *Australia II* approached the committee boat, with victory within their grasp, the Australians sat tense and silent, frightened in the best traditions of superstitious sailors that any false move might somehow bring the mast tumbling down and allow Conner to sneak by. In those last few moments, one man did succumb to what must have been a dreadful desire to take a peek at the approaching line. The port grinder, John Longley, crept to the weather side of the boat so that he could peer around the headsail. He crept back and whispered to Brian Richardson: "I think we're going to win the America's Cup." They were the words that everyone wanted to hear and yet no one wanted to hear . . . just in case something went wrong. Longley was clobbered into silence. Even when they finally heard the boom of the cannon and the white smoke drifted past, there was a strange, stunned silence. John Bertrand covered his face with both hands. Colin Beashel remembers it being a deeply emotional moment. "No one spoke for a while," he said. "We all just sat there looking at each other, some of us grinning, some crying. I remember there were quite a few tears. I certainly let a few go. Hughie Treharne was the first to speak, "I don't believe it. We've actually won it." There was a bit of back slapping and hand shaking, but then our thoughts turned back to the boat. We knew we had to get the gear off her quickly because a great mob of spectators was heading our way. Somehow we just wanted to be together then, just the crew and Bondy and Warren and Ben. We were very close, like brothers. I think that closeness is one of the things I'll remember most about that Cup campaign."

After a delay of almost an hour, the yacht race of the century was underway. Although *Australia II* lost the start, the margin was only eight seconds and everyone settled down for a good race. On *Australia II*, the 'switch was on', this was the one to win.

But by the 5th mark, things were looking pretty dismal for the Australians. *Liberty* was 57 seconds ahead and in a two-boat race this margin is almost unsurmountable. Even the most cock-eyed optimist was beginning to doubt *Australia II*'s ability to catch up.

While a record spectator fleet of 2000 boats looked on and a Coast Guard helicopter shepherded stragglers off the course, *Australia II* staged one of the greatest comebacks in sporting history. The Australians gambled on better wind on the right side of the downwind leg and with spinnaker flying they parted company with the Americans.

Australia II caught *Liberty* on the downwind leg and led her around the bottom mark by 21 seconds. But it was not due to better breeze alone. She used a more effective spinnaker and sailed a more direct course to the buoy thus making up 78 seconds in the 4.5 mile downwind leg.

But Dennis Conner refused to give up. He threw 47 tacks on the last leg of the race and almost succeeded in drawing Bertrand dangerously close to the wall of spectator boats near the finish. But Bertrand covered his every move in a tacking duel that thrilled spectators now including a television audience of over a million in Australia alone.

Finally, Bertrand broke from his defensive duel with Conner and headed for
the finish. The American boat could do nothing now but follow. After another
agonising five minutes, *Australia II* crossed the line 41 seconds ahead of *Liberty*
winning the 7th race and the America's Cup.

Radio and television announcers at the scene were virtually speechless. The Australians had done the impossible and it was difficult to tell whether it was the crew or the spectators that was the more deleriously happy. Once again the spectator fleet mobbed *Australia II* but this time their achievement was absolute.

It was sunset by the time the victorious Australians and their fleet of supporters were settled down enough to head back to Newport. With the boxing kangaroo flapping on her forestay, *Australia II* leaves the race area triumphant as millions of early-rising Australians watch via satellite.

CELEBRATIONS
AND HOMECOMING

AUSTRALIA II and her crew came home to a heroes' welcome the likes of which Australia has not seen since the triumphant return of her troops from the battlefields of both world wars.

Every man, woman and child was caught up in a whirlwind of national pride. Green and gold ribbons, the national colours, the colours of the wattle, were proudly flown from every home, every car, anything that would support them. Australian flags blossomed right across the country and for the first time in a long while Australians had something they could smile about, all share with one another.

In a country just 200 years young, a country cut-off from the ancient tradition, the culture, the heritage of the old world, Australians often look to their sporting heroes and their achievements to bring them the international attention they would otherwise not receive. International ignorance of all things Australian with the exception of kangaroos and koala 'bears' has long been a source of anxiety at home. *Australia II's* win focused world attention, if only briefly, on the men from Down Under. People in the Old World were entitled to wonder how a country of 15 million (the population of Shanghai) had been able to produce a yacht of such sophistication it had outsailed the very best that the United States, the world's most powerful nation, could put up.

The answer lay not merely with the winged keel although certainly that was of critical importance; and nor did it lie with Alan Bond or John Bertrand, but rather with a close-knit combination of a thousand and one essentially Australian factors all pulling together. When things looked grimmest for the Australians in Newport, Alan Bond invoked the hallowed names of Anzac and Gallipoli to describe the fighting spirit of his men. It was an apt description. Their welcome home was in keeping with that great tradition.

THERE MAY HAVE BEEN a stunned silence with tears of joy aboard *Australia II*, but from the moment she crossed the line, there were scenes of wild pandemonium, not only in Newport, but right throughout Australia. In a voice cracked with emotion, I yelled the news into a handkerchief-covered microphone to ABC listeners across the length and breadth of Australia. "We've won . . . we've won the America's Cup . . . we've won the America's Cup!". It was a glorious, jubilant moment, looking over that mad scrambling fleet, all tearing and racing to get close to the boat, to the men who had at that very moment made history. A great flight of green and gold balloons took to the air from a spectator ferry and flew across to *Australia II* which was by now yawning and rolling like a toy boat in a maelstrom. Some of the balloons settled in the water and looked for all the world like that great Australian party treat for kids: hundreds and thousands. And indeed the party had begun. On the press boat, my four bottles of the finest French champagne were set upon and devoured by a pack of wolfish journalists. I finished up with half a plastic cup to offer my own toast. Bubbly never tasted quite so good. Alan Bond, Warren Jones and Ben Lexcen, who had sat so grim faced during the darkest moments of that final race, now leapt into an inflatible dinghy and dashed through the boiling sea to join the crew. They scrambled on board, and there were more hugs, handshakes and raised-fist salutes.

Liberty, the vanquished defender, was left behind and for the moment at least, apparently forgotten as the world turned its attention toward *Australia II*. Later, when Dennis Conner came aboard *Australia II*'s tender, *Black Swan*, he approached Sir James Hardy, the only man he recognised. "Jim," he said through tears, "I did my best. I did my best." And so he had. Conner had sailed magnificently throughout the summer. He had taken a demonstrably slower boat and pushed her to within an ace of retaining the Cup. Looking back on the 1983 campaign, Conner said it was an event in which virtually everything went right for the *Liberty* campaign, except the result. Halfway up the last beat of the last race of the America's Cup final, I still thought we were going to somehow pull the rabbit out of the hat,"
252

he said. "The idea of losing, actually crossing the line behind John Bertrand and the Australians, just wasn't part of our program for the Cup."

Conner, The Programmed Man, the man who had devoted three years of his life to retaining the Cup, the cold calculating "killer Conner" of legend was now revealed as a very humble, very ordinary human being. And yet he was still courageous enough to come to the final press conference. He did so alone and unassisted by the men or the club he had fought so hard for. Perhaps he wanted it that way. Losing the America's Cup was a very personal thing for Dennis Conner.

Australia II was well over an hour under tow back to Newport. She was surrounded by at least a thousand boats who stuck with her all the way back in the gathering dusk. A vast crowd had gathered at Castle Hill, the rocky bluff overlooking the entrance to Narragansett Bay and the run up to Newport's historic harbour. There were cannons and fire works and flags and bunting. The whole world seemed to be mad with the delirium of the Australian win. And it was extraordinary for an Australian to see the extent of genuine American support for the triumph of the Aussie underdogs. Ordinary people in their thousands came down to the Newport waterfront to continue the celebration as the Australians edged their way into their berth through a maze of boats. Everything and anything that could float seemed to have found its way into that hitherto sacred pen. There were kayaks and canoes, surfboards and dinghies. People swam fully clothed, while others simply stood and gaped in the twelve-deep crowd. The air was wet with champagne showers. Up above the dock, on the deck of the suspended *Challenge 12*, stood a mob of madly excited Australians with monster jeroboams and magnums of bubbly that were shaken and sprayed down on those of us lucky enough to push through to the water's edge. No one cared. We were all about to be honoured with a ringside seat to yet another chapter in the history of the Cup, the unveiling of that fantastic winged keel. A mighty chant arose from the crowd and grew into a wild command. "Let's see the keel . . . let's see the keel," they yelled until eventually a beaming

Alan Bond leapt up on the stern of *Black Swan* and gave a signal like an orchestra conductor commanding a curtain rise.

Up, up, up it inched like a strip tease artiste, gradually revealing more and more of that curved white underbody that had remained hidden behind those green canvas skirts for so long. And as it rose, there was a growing crescendo of cheers and applause, as first the keel's radical forward sloping edge was revealed, then the short thick trunk, beautifully tapered in an aerodynamic curve, like a powerful glistening aircraft wing. Finally the tips of the wings broke the surface, exposed to the world under the glare of arc lights and a thousand popping flash guns. The keel looked for all the world like a beautiful living thing, a sea creature from the very depths of the ocean, suddenly risen up to see for itself what all the noise and fuss was about. It was a strange, almost irridescent blue and white, a camouflage of colours to mask its true shape from aerial photographers who might have captured it on a clear day. The crowd went completely mad when they saw it revealed. Like squealing children at a bumper Christmas party, they had waited impatiently through so many months for this particular package to be unwrapped. All the hassles with the NYYC, all the intrigue with the Canadian divers, all the accusations and innuendo about Dutch designers had created an aura about this winged keel, a mystique that drew people forward and compelled them to reach out and touch it. They stroked it and kissed it and hugged it. One man paddled in on a surfboard, dressed in a tuxedo, carrying a bottle of champagne and a glass. He poured a toast, plonked the bottle on the left hand wing and raised his glass in salute.

While all this pandemonium surrounded them, the crew and all the men and women who had supported them, stood about beaming and soaking up the success they had earned. The crew were of course overjoyed, and yet I thought they remained remarkably self-contained and in-control. There were no wild excesses. No one was tossed in the water. "There was no yahooing," Colin Beashell said, "because that was not our style. We wanted to get the boat settled down and then head home for a couple of quiet drinks among ourselves. We were a very close-knit crew." But before they could get away, there was a press conference to attend. Alan Bond paraded every member of his squad, the racing crew and all the back up men and women who had played such a vital role in *Australia II*'s success. Warren Jones introduced them all one by one, from skipper John Bertrand on down to the most junior of the sailmakers. They all got a mention. That was consistent with Bond's policy throughout the Cup campaign. He never announced the names of his crew. So far as the Australians were concerned, they were all "crew." That drew the whole group into one very close, family style unit that became protective not only of the boat, but also of each other.

After the media had their questions answered, the crew made their way out into Thames Street, through yet another crowd of applauding on-lookers. They smiled and waved, then climbed on their bicycles and mopeds and went home. Walking back to my own Newport home, along darkened Spring Street, I spotted the tall, slightly stooped figure of Ben Lexcen and his wife Yvonne, walking alone, arm in arm back to the solitude of their own apartment. The man who had broken the America's Cup's magic spell wanted nothing more than that.

Meanwhile, back in Australia, the entire country seemed to have come to a standstill. The morning traffic jam that usually chokes the Sydney Harbour Bridge came almost an hour late as tens of thousands of people stayed home to watch the final moments of the race on television, and, at the same time, listen to the commentary on radio. At the Royal Perth Yacht Club, Prime Minister Hawke turned up to be pummelled and doused with champagne by a wildly enthusiastic mob. And in cities and towns across Australia, corks popped and complete strangers grinned and hugged and spoke to each other in a manner unprecedented since the end of World War II. *Australia II*'s win brought Australians together, it gave them a common focus, a talking point. David had slain Goliath. It was a star to which everyone could hitch their wagon.

The celebrations went on in Australia for

months. In October, the Western Australian Premier declared a statewide holiday, *Australia II* Day, in an imaginitive tribute to the people involved. Many of the greats of Australian sport gathered together in Perth for celebrations that went on all day, and over 400,000 people were reported to have turned out from Fremantle to Perth to welcome the crew home. Then there were civic receptions and keys to the city, and medallions and presentations and speeches and handshakes. All Australia, it seemed, wanted to say, "well done."

In November, *Australia II* herself came home. To the delight of tens of thousands of people, she was put on display at Sydney's vast Entertainment Centre fully rigged with mainsail and tri-radial jib. It was an eerie sight to see the great yacht standing there unassisted by any props or scaffolding. The entire boat was balanced on the amazing wings that carried her to victory in Newport. It is planned to take *Australia II* around Australia to show the people, the millions who have perhaps never seen a yacht, let alone a 12-metre, but who nevertheless supported her, what the America's Cup winner looks like. There are plans too for

the Cup itself to make a national tour, travelling from city to city under the protection of armed security escorts.

Gradually, after all the tumult and shouting faded away, Australians began to wonder about the future of the Cup. How would they keep it? How much would it cost? Who would pay for it?

The Western Australian government very generously announced that they would assist the Royal Perth Yacht Club in the defence. They appointed a former Commodore, Noel Semmens, who also served as WA Director of Tourism to liase between the government and the club. The initial plan calls for the construction of an entirely new marina complex at Fremantle's Success Harbour, one that could cope with the demands of 12-metres, but would be used as a community boating facility as well.

Crew houses will be built or found, sail lofts created and marina space provided for the thousands of spectator boats expected to make their way to the Cup competition. Western Australia is determined to show the world, and some of its more strident east coast critics, that it can and will put on a good show.

At Christie's, the party started before the fleet arrived back in Newport, but everyone eagerly awaited *Australia II*'s grand entrance. The two billboard cartoons by Paul Rigby displayed near the bar all summer and intended as light-hearted humour now appeared to be prophetic. Australia had won!

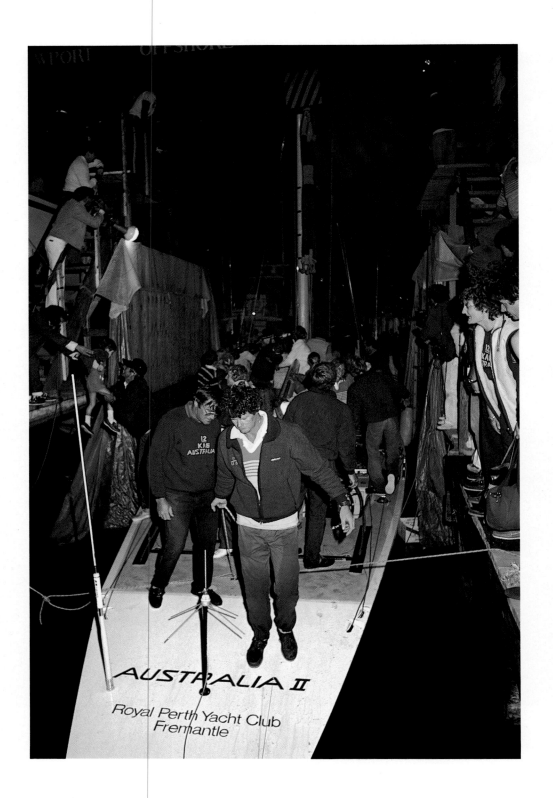

Australia II arrived back at her slip after sunset, but the gathering darkness probably intensified the high spirits. Champagne at first flowed freely, then it was sprayed in great fountains over the multitude of well-wishers. But no one cared — this was a moment to be savoured only once in a lifetime.

Black Swan first mate Newton Roberts celebrates with his wife Diane and Ben Lexcen whose 'breakthrough' boat had just set a new standard in 12-metre design. Alan Bond, the boy from Perth, had finally set the record straight after nine years of disappointment.

All the pressure of the summer of constant training and testing was over. Rasa Bertrand hugs husband John oblivious to the glare of scores of television lights and John and Alan leave the boat as it is about to be raised from the water.

The final press conference was triumphant for the Australians. Alan Bond presented each of the crew to the world's press and in turn was barraged by their questions. Dennis Conner came by himself and, although beaten, demonstrated his outstanding sportsmanship — he will no doubt be in Fremantle for the first Australian defence hoping to bring the Cup back to the NYYC.

The normally calm and collected Warren Jones had a momentary lapse after the final race and berated a fellow countryman from another syndicate. In doing so, he became the final recipient of the infamous 'red card', awarded to crewmen who fail to keep the team standard for self-control. (pages 41 and 42).

The Royal Perth Yacht Club set the scene for the rest of the country. Over a million Australians stayed up most of the night watching the race and they weren't to be denied their victory celebrations. Many didn't get to work until midday and some didn't make it at all, but it was a day no one will ever forget.

The gathered crowd shouted in unison for Alan Bond to unveil the marvellous keel. "Let's see the keel" they chanted, and finally Bondy succumbed. The canvas skirts were raised and there it was. John Longley remembered the scene well. "They were going around touching it like it had some magical powers", he recalled. And perhaps it did. It has certainly set a new design parameter in 12-metre yachts; one that is certain to be followed by all entrants in the first Australian defence in the summer of 1986-87 in Fremantle.

Meanwhile in Australia . . .

LOCAL BOY ROB BROWN
WITH HELP OF ALAN
BOND WINS AMERICA'S CUP
AUSTRALIA II 4
LIBERTY 3

As the day wore on, the mood continued. The afternoon newspapers splashed the story across their front pages and while Alan Bond flourishes his gold-plated spanner, syndicate sponsor Westpac shows its enthusiasm for the victory.

On the morning after the Australian victory, the New York Yacht Club turned its most famous keepsake over to the Royal Perth Yacht Club. The presentation was made on the steps of Marble House, the old Vanderbilt mansion at Newport and graciousness, with a little humour, was the order of the day.

Shortly after the America's Cup was presented, NYYC Commodore Robert Stone, Jr. gave Ben Lexcen a special gift. This old Plymouth hubcap was in response to a remark made by Lexcen where he said if *Australia II* won the Cup he'd take the auld mug onto New York's West 44th Street, run over it with a steam roller, and make it 'America's Plate.'

Australia II and *Challenge 12* are packed up ready for the three day tow back to New York. Both yachts, plus the tender *Black Swan* were then loaded on a ship for the return trip to Australia.

FOLLOWING PAGE Perth welcomes the *Australia II* crew.

Starting at the Fremantle Town Hall, the parade took the entire *Australia II* crew
over to the Esplanade in Perth for a huge celebration.

Entertainment for the huge crowd was non-stop. The crew was introduced; television, film and stage stars performed and the America's Cup unveiled. The celebrations, which ran for most of the day and into the night, were beamed to an enormous television audience across Australia.

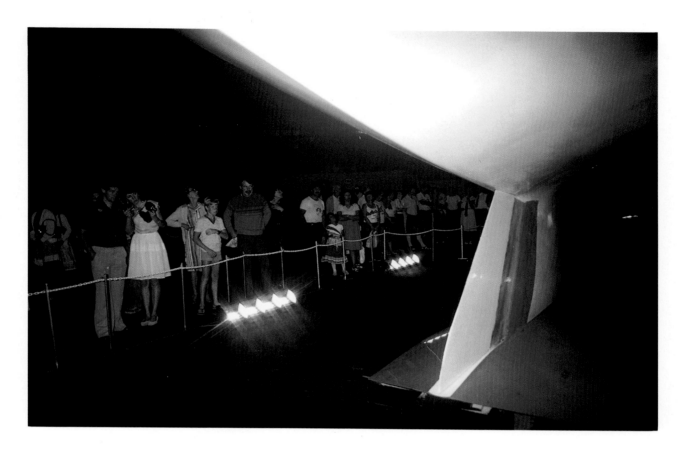

Australia II arrived back home in November and made her first public appearance at Sydney's new Entertainment Centre. She was an immediate hit, perched firmly on her winged keel in the middle of the arena with her giant mast reaching up through a small opening in the ceiling. Over 60,000 people filed past her in the first two weeks and she promptly had her run extended for another few weeks.

EPILOGUE

Now that we have won the America's Cup, the question on all Australian lips is, can we hold on to it? The answer is yes, but with a pretty hefty proviso that has everything to do with the simple and yet strangely elusive quality known as national unity. When *Australia II* won the America's Cup there was a tremendous, not to say astonishing outpouring of that very substance. It was something quite strange for most Australians. We are not an outwardly demonstrative people like say the Italians. And yet given the right moment we can and do rise to the occasion. If that national spirit can be channelled into a Cup defence campaign then I believe we will retain the auld mug. Syndicates from Queensland, New South Wales and South Australia are well advanced with plans to fight for the right to defend the cup on behalf of the Royal Perth Yacht Club. Alan Bond will of course be in there fighting too. But it would be a mistake to imagine that Bondy can do it on his own. We face the staggering prospect of three American challengers as well as others from Britain, Italy and possibly New Zealand and Japan. To rest on our laurels, to allow Alan Bond to shoulder the entire burden alone, would be to invite the certain loss of the Cup. These views are shared by *Australia II's* designer Ben Lexcen. Lexcen warned that an "unselfish" approach was required for Australia to hold the Cup.

"Yes, Bondy won it," he said, "but he can't hold on to it on his own. We need other, equally determined people to go out there and fight for the right to defend it. Whoever wants to be in this Cup defence effort has got to declare themselves and get their act together within a year. It's going to take at least three years to get the whole thing right, to get the boats designed and built, to get the right people around us and to make all the sails and rigs."

LEXCEN ALSO WARNED that really tough, no-holds-barred competition between the Cup defence candidates was essential. "These boats will have to be dedicated to each other's destruction," he said. "They will have to hone the same sort of killer instincts the American syndicates have always had.

They will have to go out and battle each other day after day, otherwise that Cup will go straight back to America: that's my prediction. There's no way a friendly, sweetheart defence can retain the Cup; it's just not possible. That's where the Americans went wrong last time: they had a defence that was so sweethearted by the NYYC allowing it to do this, that, and the other they ended up selecting the wrong boat. They chose their favourite instead of the one that was actually the best and they lost."

Royal Perth, he said, had a very big job ahead of it. It had to come up with a set of trials which would be "very rigorous, very testing." "They can't be trials in which boats are picked by opinion," he said. "There has to be conclusive proof that one boat is better than another. There cannot be any sentimental favourites."

The first Australian defence of the Cup is expected to be held in 1987 in the moderate to strong south-westerly sea breezes characteristic of the Indian Ocean in February, March and April. The courses will most likely start four miles offshore at the Fairway Buoy, a bell marker similar to the America's Cup buoy off Newport, which signals the approach to Fremantle Harbour.

There is no such thing as a gentle breeze off Fremantle. As soon as the vast hinterland has heated up — usually by midday — the cool south-westerly is sucked in from the sea. It brings so much relief it's become known as the Fremantle Doctor. The sea breeze produces a long medium-sized swell over the deep waters of Gage Roads.

The Cup courses off Fremantle will remain exactly the same as they were off Newport with the start always into the wind, a starboard reaching leg under spinnaker, a gybe, then a port reach under spinnaker, a fourth leg into the wind, a square run under spinnaker and the final leg to windward to finish. The distance will remain 24.5 miles.

The heavier air off Fremantle will force designers into a complete reassessment of the best shapes for 12-metre yachts. The boats are likely to be longer on the waterline, carry a smaller sail area and have a greater displacement. *Australia II's* win with her winged keel and the IYRU's subsequent vindication of Ben Lexcen's design development means that every new 12-metre in Fremantle for the first Australian defence will have to incorporate some variation of it. No one can afford to come to those Cup races without wings and still be competitive.

The America's Cup summer of '86-'87 promises a feast of great match racing and a chance for all Australia to play host to some of the world's finest yachtsmen plus the tens of thousands of international visitors drawn to the great regatta.

It will be hard, very hard, to fight off those challenges. But that is precisely what the America's Cup has always been about. Yachting's supreme challenge hasn't changed. It has simply shifted from the fog shrouded waters off Rhode Island Sound, down into the bright sunshine of the Indian Ocean.

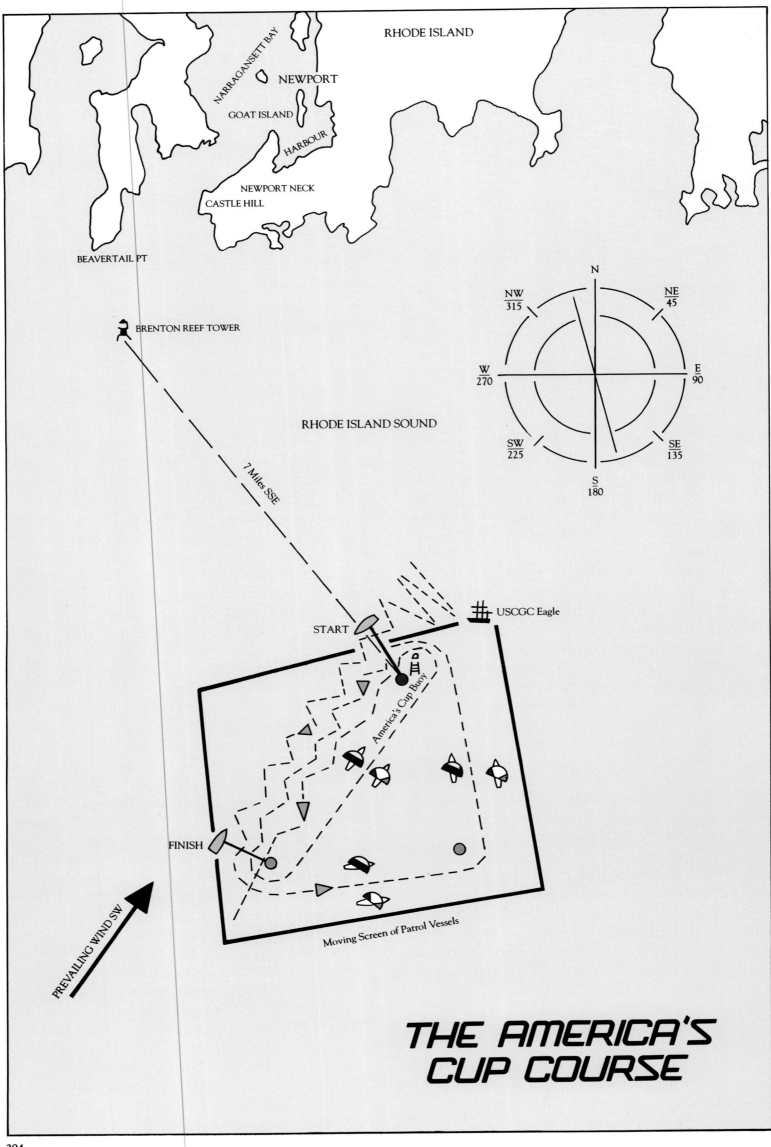

RHODE ISLAND

NARRAGANSETT BAY

NEWPORT

GOAT ISLAND

HARBOUR

NEWPORT NECK

CASTLE HILL

BEAVERTAIL PT

BRENTON REEF TOWER

RHODE ISLAND SOUND

N
180

NW
315

NE
45

W
270

E
90

SW
225

SE
135

S
180

7 Miles SSE

START

USCGC Eagle

America's Cup Buoy

FINISH

Moving Screen of Patrol Vessels

PREVAILING WIND SW

THE AMERICA'S CUP COURSE

DECK PLAN

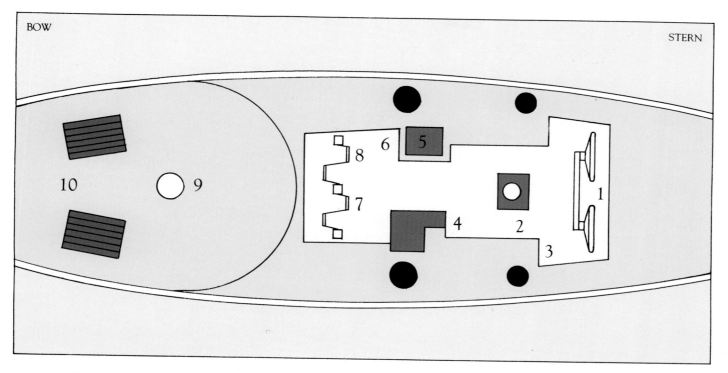

BOW

STERN

1 HELMSMAN 2 TACTICIAN 3 NAVIGATOR 4 MAIN SHEET TRIMMER 5 & 6 HEADSAIL TRIMMER 7 & 8 WINCH GRINDERS
9 MAST MAN 10 BOWMAN

THE AUSTRALIA II TEAM

TOP ROW
DAMIAN FEWSTER *Bowman* PHIL JUDGE *Skipper, Tender* SCOTT McALLISTER *Bowman*

SECOND ROW
NEWTON ROBERTS *1st Mate, Tender* KEN O'BRIEN *Head Sailmaker* LAURIE HAYDEN *Sport Psychologist* MIKE QUILTER *Sailmaker*
COL BEASHEL *Mainsheet Trimmer* KEN JUDGE *Trimmer* KEN BEASHEL *Maintenance Supervisor* DAVE WALLACE *Maintenance*

FIRST ROW
STEVE HARRISON *Maintenance* ROB BROWN *Trimmer* GLENN READ *Computer Technician* JOHN FITZHARDINGE *Race Committee/Yacht Rigger*
WILL BAILLIEU *Grinder* PETER COSTELLO *Grinder/Sewerman* BRIAN RICHARDSON *Grinder* MARK REID *Chase Boat Skipper*
TED SILBEREISEN *Sailmaker* PHIL SMIDMORE *Mastman* DAVID REES *Sailmaker*

SEATED
ALISON BAKER *Secretary* MIKE FLETCHER *Sailing Coach* JOHN LONGLEY *Project Manager/Grinder* JOHN BERTRAND *Skipper*
ALAN BOND *Syndicate Chairman* WARREN JONES *Syndicate Managing Director* HUGH TREHARNE *Tactician* GRANT SIMMER *Navigator*
SKIP LISSIMAN *Trimmer* LESLEIGH GREEN *Public Relations*

ABSENT
SIR JAMES HARDY *Sailing Adviser/Director* BEX LEXCEN *Designer* TOM SCHNACKENBURG *Sail Designer*

CREDITS

EDITOR Andy Park
TEXT Bruce Stannard
DESIGN AND PRODUCTION MANAGER John Stewart
ART DIRECTION AND COVER DESIGN
Andrew Barnum - Lissa Mendelsohn Barnum
FINISHED ART Deborah Matterson
FINANCIAL CONSULTANTS Australian Bank, Ltd.
ACCOUNTANTS Coopers & Lybrand
LEGAL ADVISOR Barron Stevenson & Buddin
PICTURE AGENCY Talentbank
PHOTOSETTING Setup
Australia II TYPEFACE Face, The Type Workshop
PUBLISHED BY Joyce Childress Management, Pty. Ltd.
PRINTED BY Dai Nippon Printing Company, Tokyo.

PHOTOGRAPHER'S CREDITS
(and page numbers)

Bill Bachman	35
Rob Brown	36-37, 72, 75, 90, 114, 116-117, 136B, 158, 164A, 171A, 271B, 287B
Peter Carrette	100, 115, 166-167, 219A, 224-225, 230, 244, 255B, 268-269, 276A
Graham Collopy	29
Michael Coyne	12-13, 280-281, 283B, 284-285, 290-291
Tom Edkins	239, 266-267
Roger Garwood	30-31, 32B-33B, 282, 283A, 286, 287A
Arthur Grace	57B, 58, 68-69B, 82-83A, 84-85, 92-93, 112B, 122, 137, 183A, 186-187, 200, 242, 245, 264
Barry Gray	70, 159, 218
Lesleigh Green	80-81, 97, 277
Gail Grey	32A-33A
Guy Gurney	188-189
Carolyn Johns	219B, 247A, 270-271, 274B, 275
Phil Judge	99
Peter Kinder	24-28
Skip Lissiman	279A
John Longley	71B, 112A, 161, 165, 173A, 175, 231, 240A, 278
Lindsay Matthews	254A-255A, 286-287
Dan Nerney	16-17, 54-55, 66-67, 69A, 76-79, 87, 123, 176-177, 179-181, 189, 191-193, 210, 234-236
Peter Oossanen	20-21, 56-57A, 155, 172, 198-199
Barbara Pyle	4-5, 8, 10, 14, 46-51, 53, 59, 63-65, 73B, 86, 94-95, 98, 104-105, 110-111, 124-125, 127-129, 174, 214-216, 237-238, 248-249, 262-263, 272A, 274A, 276B
Tom Ragland	6-7, 52, 102-103, 106-107, 138, 140-145, 147, 150-53, 156-157, 204-207, 211, 220-221, 227-229, 232, 243
Mark Reid	136A, 279B
Sally Samins	44-45, 62, 73A, 74, 91B, 101, 118-119, 126, 130-133, 139, 154, 160, 162-163, 178, 182, 183B, 194-197, 202-203, 212-213, 217, 226, 240B, 247B, 256-257, 260-261, 265
Hugh Smith	2-3, 134-135, 148, 184-185, 209, 241
Allan Stannard	246
Bruce Stannard	71A, 83B, 88-89, 146, 170 171B, 233B
Susan Stannard	113, 164B, 190, 201, 208, 233A
Anthony Tiere	34, 294
Grace Trofa	96, 149, 173B, 259
Graham Young	60-61, 91A, 168-169, 258, 272B, 273A

SPONSORS FOR AMERICA'S CUP CHALLENGE 1983:

ACTA Pty. Limited
ACTO Structures Pty. Ltd.
ACI Group
Advance Australia Challenge America's Cup
American Airlines
ANZ Bank
Australian National Industries Limited
Australian Posters
Berri Fruit Juices Co-operative Ltd.
Bisley Arms Company
Mr. P. Briggs
C.H.E.C. (Melbourne) Pty. Ltd.
Chuck Roast Equipment Inc.
Citizen Watches Australia Pty. Ltd.
Clubknit
G.J. Coles & Co. Ltd.
Comalco
Comalco Aluminium Supply
Corporate Television Productions
Dallhold Investments Pty. Ltd.
Darcy McManus & Masius Pty. Ltd.
Data General Australia Pty. Ltd.
David Jones Limited
Dunlop Footwear

Epicraft Consolidated Chemicals
Esso Australia Limited
Europe Strength Foods
Ford Motor Company of Australia Ltd.
Fremantle Port Authority
J. Gadsden Australia Limited
Hoechst Roussell Pharmaceuticals
Mr. M.R.H. Holmes a Court
HySport International Pty. Ltd.
Jackson Graham Moore & Partners
The Jean Machine
Kim's Bar & Cafe
Lewmar Marine Ltd.
Line 7
Motorolla
News Ltd.
North Sails
OPSM
Otis Elevator Company Ltd.
Parker & Parker
Perth Fibre Box
Peters Group of Companies
Plastimo
Port of Melbourne Authority

Price Waterhouse
Project Hire
Qantas Airways Ltd.
Rank Xerox (Australia) Pty. Ltd.
Roger Garwood Photography
Ronstan Marine Equipment Pty. Ltd.
Rumward Ltd.
Sharp Corporation
Solo Marine Pty. Limited
Spinnaker Club
Sports Skins International
Stateships
Stubbies Pty. Ltd.
STW Channel 9
The Swan Brewery Company Ltd.
3M Australia
Trans Australia Airlines
Turner Graphics
Waltons Bond Limited
West Australian Newspapers
Western Underwriters Pty. Ltd.
Westfield Limited
Westpac Banking Corporation
Whitemans Brick Limited

*And a special thanks to Ray Needham for believing that a book
on Australia II was possible even when the score was 1-3.*

The publisher would like to thank the staff and crew of Australia II for their moral support, inside information and boundless sense of humour.